RANGER UP!

TRUE STORIES OF NATIONAL PARK SERVICE
PROTECTION RANGERS

Richard E. (Rick) Brown

authorHOUSE®

AuthorHouse™
1663 Liberty Drive
Bloomington, IN 47403
www.authorhouse.com
Phone: 1-800-839-8640

First published by AuthorHouse 2/1/2010

ISBN: 978-1-4490-1779-8 (e)
ISBN: 978-1-4490-1778-1 (sc)

Library of Congress Control Number: 2010900481

Printed in the United States of America
Bloomington, Indiana
This book is printed on acid-free paper.

For my family Linda, Charlie and Jessica — true rangers at heart
And
To all the dedicated National Park Rangers

FOREWORD

In "Ranger Up" my good friend and respected colleague Rick Brown has not only succeeded in telling a number of wonderful stories from his own career, but helped readers better understand what it really means to be a National Park Protection Ranger.

The general public quite often has a romantic, but somewhat naïve view of what being a Ranger actually entails. Most view the Ranger as an iconic figure, skilled and knowledgeable; working in a beautiful park setting, but know little else about the actual details of the work. Rick Brown does an excellent job of explaining the passion, training, skill and attitude it takes to be successful in this profession and the often arduous and dangerous working conditions under which all Rangers are expected to perform. His stories will amaze you, entertain you, make you mad, and make you cry.

Rick's book deserves to be read for another reason. While all Rangers have some good stories to tell, very few achieve the level of competence and excellence in as many of the essential Ranger disciplines (resource education, public relations, law enforcement, emergency medical services, search and rescue, firefighting and complex incident management) as Rick achieved during his 30 year career with the National Park Service. Few win Valor Awards. Very few are chosen to lead one of the National Park Service's All-Risk Incident Management Teams, and very few are selected to receive the National Harry Yount Award, the highest peer recognition in the protection ranger profession. With the support of a wonderful family, Rick has done all of these things, and as is clear in the book, has just as much passion for the mission of the National Park Service and for being a Ranger as he ever did.

I have had the privilege of working with Rick in two parks; the Buffalo National River and at Great Smoky Mountains National Park. We have run rivers, rappelled off cliffs, crawled through caves, fought fires and made arrests together and I would trust him with my life in any circumstance. Rick is truly a Ranger's Ranger – so Ranger Up – read his book. You'll be glad you did.

JIM NORTHUP
Superintendent of Pictured Rocks National Lakeshore, and the former Chief Ranger of Great Smoky Mountains National Park

ACKNOWLEDGEMENTS:

One does not start out in life expecting to have a successful career in any job field; it takes a lot of hard work, training, mentoring and help along the way from other very talented peers, supervisors, managers and friends. Park rangers and other National Park Service employees tend to be a very clannish bunch; they work together as a team regardless of their job assignment, and help each other out along the way. Without the support of all of my fellow rangers and park employees I would not have achieved the degree of success I have in the National Park Service. I set my goals high and was able to achieve most of them, but not without the help of this true team of very special people behind me, and then only because they believed in me.

There are a few that deserve special thanks from their help in producing this book, Butch McDade - retired NPS ranger, author and friend, who offered his time and expert advice to help me over some rough spots, and rangers Bob Wightman and Steve Kloster who helped me locate some photos, support and encouragement along the way.

The group that deserves the vast majority of credit and my appreciation is my immediate and extended family. My son Charlie and daughter Jessica who endured some rough times growing up in parks, and pitched in to help where ever they could – like true rangers. To my wife Linda, who stood by me throughout the years giving her support, advice, guidance; and as my chief editor spent countless nights going blind while she corrected my grammatical errors, and endured my whining when things were not going just right. As always this book is a product of teamwork – the Brown Team rides again!

TABLE OF CONTENTS

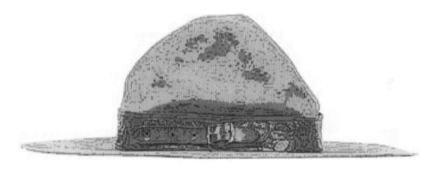

"....send a ranger"

Stephen T. Mather, the first director of the National Park Service

"Ranger UP! – Placing a ranger on point in the 'one problem one ranger' concept of the National Park Service"

INTRODUCTION

Stephen T. Mather, the first director of the National Park Service stated, "If a trail is to be blazed, send a ranger, if an animal is floundering in the snow, send a ranger, if a bear is in a hotel, send a ranger, if a fire threatens a forest, send a ranger, and if someone needs to be saved, send a ranger". In short, the park ranger has to do it all at one time or another. Park rangers are the heart and soul of the National Park Service, the glue that holds it all together. Like a parent to a child, the ranger is to the visitor and the park a combination of educator, guide, provider, nurturer, enforcer, and protector.

Some Park Rangers have very specific duties and deal almost exclusively with education and interpretation of the parks resources. These are generally the rangers that manage the park visitor centers and give interpretive walks and talks. Some have specific duties that focus all of their attention to the science and resources management field; these rangers are the wildlife managers, backcountry managers, or cultural resource managers. Other rangers have a wide variety of duties including law enforcement, search and rescue, emergency medical services, and firefighting. In addition to these four major specialties, these same rangers are often responsible for many other duties. These are the Protection Rangers.

By definition the Protection Ranger has the primary responsibility for Law Enforcement (LE), Search and Rescue (SAR), Emergency

Medical Services (EMS), and Firefighting in the parks. But depending on the particular park they are working in they may be responsible for a whole lot more. In some parks the Protection Ranger may also be responsible for other components of park management including resource management, fee management, boundary management, education/interpretation, and sometimes even that of maintenance worker.

However, in today's fast paced society the crime rate has escalated significantly across the Nation. Along with this rise in the crime rate we have also seen a significant increase in park visitation, and therefore an ever increasing incident rate in our National Parks. This makes it very difficult for a ranger to maintain proficiency, as well as the required certifications in all four of the emergency services fields.

Therefore, many Protection Rangers in the National Park Service (NPS) today are beginning to specialize. They are still required to maintain their training, certification, and proficiency in law enforcement, firefighting, SAR, and EMS, but may for instance make their specialty, or emphasis, law enforcement. When this happens those rangers become the backup cadre to pull from when a SAR, EMS or firefighting incident occurs. This actually works out pretty well, a ranger with an interest in one of these fields may become the park expert in that field; he or she takes the lead and the other rangers follow. During a typical day in the park, one minute you may be working a law enforcement incident, the next a SAR incident, and the next a fire, so everyone gets a chance to lead, and to follow. That said many rangers still prefer to "do it all, and do it well". These are the rangers that take immense pride in learning, developing, and maintaining their knowledge, skills, and abilities in all of the emergency services fields. They are the elite within an elite group, the natural leaders regardless of the type of incident. But at the same time they are also willing and able to follow, to coach, to instruct. Within the Service these rangers are known as a "Rangers Ranger", meaning of course that they are the rangers that other rangers look up to and call upon when a major incident arises.

When you compare the National Park Service to any other law enforcement or emergency response agency one of the major differences you will quickly note is the number of individuals that respond to a call. When another law enforcement or emergency service agency is dispatched to an emergency they respond in numbers; and as a general rule most LE agencies have backup available within minutes of a request. On the other hand NPS Protection Rangers typically work alone, and it's not at all unusual for their backup to be more than fifteen or more minutes away. Call a ranger and usually only one comes on the initial response. But when they get on scene you can expect to get a highly qualified, dedicated, and capable person with multiple skill sets to respond to your problem. Expect that you will get results.

During my career with the NPS one of the most frequent questions I have been asked has been "What's it like to be a ranger"? That's a difficult question to answer in just a few words. It is many things, many adventures, many feelings, many disappointments, and many fantastic experiences. This book is intended to give the reader a snapshot of what a National Park Protection Ranger actually does, what it's like to be a ranger. The book is a conglomeration of many incidents that I either personally faced, or about rangers I worked with and supervised during my thirty year career with the National Park Service. Some of these stories are humorous, some are serious, some are downright sad. Together they should provide the reader with a good answer to what it's like to be a ranger.

Over my career with the National Park Service I have worked a variety of assignments from a National Battlefield, two National Rivers, and a National Park. In addition to these permanent assignments I have also worked in detailed assignments to numerous National Parks, National Forests, National Preserves, and Reservations as an emergency worker and manager.

Over the course of my career I have had the luxury of working with and being supported by some of the most professional, caring, sensitive, capable, and skilled people in the world. These rangers and other park staff helped to mentor and direct me through my career, train me in the skills of rangering, develop me into a competent ranger, and provide me with the motivation to excel. But the group that was the most supportive throughout my life and career has been my family, there is absolutely no way I could have become the person I am without their love and support.

My wife Linda and I raised our family, our son Charlie and daughter Jessica, in the National Park Service. They grew up living in parks, working with and assisting park visitors themselves, helping in tasks around the ranger station and ranger residence, volunteering their time to help clean up the campgrounds and roadsides, and in one assignment helping to taking care of the parks' horse I used on patrol. They too were very much a part of the National Park Service.

Linda is a Registered Nurse and she often helped me in the field treating patients. When someone came to the ranger station with a medical problem she would either do the doctoring herself or help me with the treatment. She was my lifeline to the outside world; she monitored the radio and relayed messages by telephone, often serving as my only dispatcher. As a Surgery nurse at the local hospital Linda would very often end up with a patient I had just rescued or treated after a falling accident, traffic accident, shooting accident or some other type incident involving a traumatic injury. After I got an injured person to the ambulance I always made it a habit to give her a call to let her know that she was probably going to get called back to the hospital. My family has always been my greatest supporters; they have made this career long journey special.

So what about the title of this book, what is the meaning of "Ranger Up"? To me it goes back to the core of the National Park Service. Since the NPS has always been underfunded the ranger has had to learn to work understaffed, and "do more with less". From the beginning of the NPS the basic premise of rangering, has been "one problem, one ranger". That simply means that one ranger is usually dispatched to assess, or size up, the problem. Most problems are handled by the one ranger, but if more help is needed the stops are pulled out to make it happen. I think of "Ranger Up" as placing the ranger on point, get out there and check out the problem, and take whatever action is necessary to correct it. When it's used in conversation between two rangers it can also mean to toughen up, or quit gripping and get on with it. It doesn't matter that you're not feeling well, tired, sore, or haven't slept in two days, when the ranger is given the assignment it will be carried out. "Ranger Up" means the best of the best are in route to take care of a problem; positive results will quickly follow.

I've been asked on several occasions over my career 'what does being a Park Ranger mean to me', the short answer is it means many things. It means being part of the best organization in the world, working with an exceptional group of people, protecting our national treasures and taking pride in being the part of the best. But what has meant the most to me was the good feeling I have always gotten from helping people. The best way for me to answer this question is to share with the reader a thank you letter that as the District Ranger at Great Smoky Mountains National Park I received from a lady that we rescued off of the mountain after she was injured.

To give background on the incident, late on the afternoon on September 8, 2004 Park Dispatch received an emergency call from Mount LeConte Lodge. The lodge is located deep inside the park, about five miles from the nearest road, and can only be reached by hiking in. One of their lodge guests had taken a fall and had a severely fractured lower leg.

Because there is a helicopter landing area nearby the lodge we would have normally called for a medical helicopter to fly her out to the hospital. However, a major rainstorm caused by Hurricane Francis had dropped 7.5 inches of rainfall over the area over the past two days. The entire area was socked in; visibility on the mountain was near zero over Mt. LeConte. There was no way we were going to get a helicopter in to make the pickup. The forecast called for an improvement over the next few days, we would have to wait and see if a change in weather occurred. A ranger/medic was sent up to the lodge on foot to treat the patient and determine the extent of injury. He would size up the problem, and make a determination on how we were going to deal with the injury. When he arrived it was determined that the injury was a severe angulated fracture, possibly a fracture of both the tibia and fibula, and circulation to the foot was very poor. A traction splint was applied to the leg to help improve the circulation. It was decided that she would be kept overnight at the lodge with the hope that we could get the helicopter in the next morning. No such luck, the next morning the mountain was still socked in. But still hoping for a change in weather we waited until noon before finally eliminating the possibility of using the helicopter. As a backup we had dispatched a fourteen person carryout team to start up the trail to Mt. LeConte that morning, they would be called off if the helicopter could be used. Now with the helicopter out of the question the extraction literally rested on the shoulders of the carryout team.

Circulation to the leg had not improved, making irreversible damage to the limb a possibility; time was becoming a factor. The best trail for a carryout was Bull Head Trail, even though it's steep, rugged, narrow, and treacherous in a couple of places. But because of the flooding to the creeks and the treacherous rocky cliffs along other trails it was the only real option we had for a land transport. The distance from LeConte to the Bullhead Trailhead, which is located off of Cherokee Orchard Road, is 7.2 miles. The litter team had to get themselves, the litter, and all of the medical gear up to the patient, package her in the litter and carry her down to the ambulance 7.2 miles away. This was going to take everyone we had, and then some; it was also going to take all day.

About five hours after beginning their hike up to the lodge the team had the patient in the litter and was starting down the trail toward the ambulance. On this particular day I was working on one of my many administrative chores, one with a deadline that had to be completed by the end of the day. I kept my nose to the grindstone and finished that task around 2:00pm, then passed it on to the Chief Ranger and started up the trail at about 3:00pm to join the litter haul team.

The following is the letter we received from the injured lady, I'll let you decide if it answers the question of "what does being a Park Ranger mean":

THANK YOU! THANK YOU! THANK YOU! THANK YOU! THANK YOU!

Dear Rescue Teams,

I wish I had a million dollars to give each of you. I wish I could cook a special gourmet meal for you. I wish I could throw a huge party in your honor. That's how grateful I am that you sacrificed your day to rescue me from Mt. Le Conte on September 8 & 9, 2004. X-rays confirmed that both bones in my left leg were broken in several places.

During our first trip up Alum Cave then the next day down Bull Head trail, each of you was so impressive in your physical strength, your character, your sense of humor and your compassion. My spirit felt connected to yours in love and peace. That's why I could be so calm throughout the trips.

I want you to know how dearly I love you and am grateful to you. I'm committed to showing you this as long as I can. I want to join the volunteer club that you spoke of and devote a certain amount of time each year to this club to help you. I have enclosed a gift of $500 in your honor to this club as my first token of appreciation. I will continue to send monetary gifts as I am able. Since I know each of you in a small way and have your faces etched in my memory, it is easier for me to pray specifically for you, your families and your work in the Park or Lodge. I will continue to pray for you always. I have attached my story for you to read if you are so inclined to hear the cause and results of the day we spent together.

I know you realize that people you have rescued and their families are thankful to you, but you may not realize that you are also an inspiration to us. The beauty of your sacrifices on behalf of us leaves us with an indelible impression of awe and admiration. I commend you for being who you are. Your integrity is a valuable asset to the many facets of your work in the Park, and everyone who visits your Park and Lodge is benefiting so much although they may never know your behind-the-scenes work. Your spectacular teamwork was synchronized so smoothly, you made the rescue appear effortless, yet your huffs and puffs and slips and slides let me know that it was grueling labor on your part. I'm glad that none of you got hurt, except I'm sure the next day you must have seriously ached.

Special thank you to your leaders those days, Chris V████, Keith F████, Rick Brown, and Ken M████. Their compassion and tough decisions led you to accomplish your mission successfully.

Thank you a million times for being there for me when I needed you. You have my name, address and phone number, and I will be there for any of you should you ever need me.

With much love,

Beverly Hood
████████████k Lane
Hampton ████, Alabama 357██
256-53█-█████ (home)
256-6██-████ (cell)
256-7██-████ (work)   email: ████████@bellsouth.net

SETTING THE STAGE – MEMORABLE MEMORIAL WEEKEND

During my career as a National Park Ranger while working with local law enforcement and emergency services agencies I was asked on numerous occasions, "Is it always this busy in the park?" The honest answer is, it depends. Winters and off season months can be downright boring at times. Then all of a sudden you get a report of a vehicle crash, or someone takes a fall and you're off and running. The calls never stop even in the off season but they do slow down. During the off season rangers generally divert their attention to resource management, safety, training or other administrative tasks that they haven't had a chance to get to during the main visitor season. In the normal visitor season the call volume generally stays pretty steady; emergency calls or law enforcement incidents come fairly frequently. There are times however, that it gets pretty slow even during the main visitor season. That's when you have to watch out because it's like the calm before the storm and all of a sudden things can get crazy. During the Memorial Weekend, 4th of July weekend, and Labor Day Weekend rangers really earn their pay.

To give you an idea of what it can be like at times look at this example of a typical Memorial Day weekend at New River Gorge National River in 1998. The weekend started off with a "bang" on Friday evening. Rangers in the Grandview area received a report of gunshots fired in the Glade Creek

Campground. The initial report was that a vehicle had driven through the campground and fired several gunshots from a moving vehicle. Shooting incidents in the park were relatively frequent, and because of the danger and unpredictability involved in these violent incidents we usually brought lots of help. Several rangers, WV State Troopers, and Raleigh County Sheriff Deputies responded to the area to investigate the report. When we arrived on scene there was no longer any vehicle activity in the area, and the campground was quiet so we went to the campsite where the person reporting the shooting was located. Initially the reporting party (RP) said he wasn't sure who, or why the shots were fired. However, after repeated questioning of the RP and other campers in the campground we learned that there had been a very rowdy party in the campsite of the RP. Witnesses said that there had been loud arguing and what sounded like a violent fight in the campsite. They heard a vehicle speed away from the campsite and then heard several gunshots come from the vicinity of the vehicle as it was speeding away. No one in the campground was able, or more likely was willing, to give any information on the persons that had fired the shots or a description of the vehicle involved.

After it was apparent that the threat had left the area, the troopers and deputies left the area, leaving the investigation to the rangers. It was apparent from the witness statements that there probably had been shots fired in the area, but since it was dark and the shots had probably gone off into the woods there was no physical evidence, at least at this point. We had witnesses saying that shots were fired from a vehicle, but no names or description of the suspects or of the vehicle, and no physical evidence to confirm the report. We had spent about two and one half hours investigating the incident, and this is one that was going to take some follow-up over the next few days or weeks before the case could be resolved. The saving grace in the incident was no one was injured.

Saturday morning started out fairly slow. Since the commercial river outfitters usually book rafting trips heavy on these weekends they get started early at the put-in areas, especially on Saturday and Sunday. The Cunard Launch Area is one of the main put-ins because it's the beginning of the lower section through the "gorge" and the beginning of the class IV+ whitewater section (using the International Grading System for whitewater, Class I is the easiest with gentle rapids or ripples, and Class VI is the most difficult and dangerous). There is normally a tremendous amount of commercial river traffic trying to squeeze into a relatively tiny space along the river, so rangers spent the morning managing the put-in operation. At the time there were twenty three commercial outfitters on this section of the river, and as the locals like to say "it's a class six bus ride down the Cunard Road, to run a class five river". The saying is pretty darn accurate, even though the road had been improved some since my arrival at New River in 1985. At that time it was a very steep, narrow, winding, unpaved, and rutted mud hole. Each of the twenty three outfitters would generally have several forty to sixty passenger buses going into and out of the two mile section of the Cunard Access Road, disgorging rafts and passengers at the river access at the bottom. The buses were typically old retired school buses that had be pressed back into service and many were held together with not much more than baling wire and duct tape. It wasn't unusual to see buses broken down on the side of the road with brake problems, engine failure, and broken axles.

Going down the narrow, winding, rutted, rocky and very steep road was an accident waiting to happen; we always prayed it wouldn't happen, but at the same time we stayed prepared. Not only was the road treacherous, but it was too narrow for two buses going in the opposite direction to pass in most of the two mile stretch. There was a lot of backing up, followed by cursing and sometimes fights. To help remedy this most outfitters equipped the buses with CB radios to communicate their location on the road, and on busy days sometimes a person was positioned at the top and bottom to act as traffic controllers.

Not only was the bus traffic on the road a problem, but on these busy weekends it was utter chaos at the launch area. Imagine twenty three commercial outfitters; all putting on at least ten rafts with eight to ten passengers in each. Some of the larger companies were putting on as many as fifty or more rafts. On a busy day there would be over two thousand boaters launching at Cunard. Not much fun for the rangers that had to manage the put-in operation, then pull up stakes and do the same thing at the take-out at Fayette Station. We would normally try to put several rangers at Cunard early in the morning to help get a handle on things, and then they would move out into other areas of the park. The section of the New River within the park boundaries is fifty two miles long, and to get from one area to another you had to leave the park and travel on County and State roads. Besides the New River the park also manages the Gauley River NRA, Meadow River NSR, and Bluestone NSR; it could be a daunting and challenging task at times with the limited number of rangers. Sometimes having extra rangers in one area worked to our advantage, sometimes it didn't work out quite so well. This Saturday started out slow with the normal chaos of managing the put-in, and then the calls began to come in. And all of a sudden it jumped up a notch, like WORP speed.

On Saturday morning the launch operation was going pretty well at Cunard. There were some testy times trying to keep the outfitters who were competing for the launch ramp to "play nice". It was almost 11:00am and for the most part all was going pretty smoothly (now remember what I said about the "quiet before the storm"?). All of a sudden the "river drums began to beat" loudly. That means that the outfitter telegraph kicked in, bus drivers were shouting on the radio that there was a "BUS OVER THE SIDE OF THE ROAD" near the top of Cunard Road. They immediately passed the report on to the rangers at the launch area and rangers began to respond. I had just left Cunard about twenty minutes before the report came in and was only about five miles away. I turned around and headed back to the accident scene. When I arrived about fifteen minutes later I found that a sixty passenger bus had rolled over the non-existent shoulder and was on its side about eight feet down the steep embankment. Luckily large trees had caught the bus before it continued over the embankment or it would have continued down the steep embankment another fifty to sixty feet; the trees had saved lives. Everyone was already off of the bus when I arrived. The bus seemed fairly stable for now. I interviewed the driver and found out that he had just unloaded a full load of passengers at the put-in and was traveling out the road when the accident occurred. According to the driver he had been forced off the road by speeding vehicles moving downhill on a very narrow section of the road. Luckily the only people on board were the driver and a driver trainee and there were no injuries.

Now we had to deal with the congestion caused by the accident. There were about eight buses still at the Cunard bottom that were trying to get out and they had passengers to pick up at the take out at Fayette Station. The outfitters were panicking, and since the launch "window" had not yet ended there were buses stacking up at the top of the road trying to get down to the put-in at Cunard. The end of the overturned bus was sticking out into the road, blocking buses from getting up or down the road – a real stalemate. It may have been possible to barely squeeze a bus through the gap, but it would have been really close, and the consequences would have been severe. If a bus tried to pass it may have hit the bus, pushing the bus further over the hill and caused it to roll, or the passing bus could have gotten lodged between the rolled bus and the trees on the opposite side of the road. We closed the road until we could see if the tow truck could remove the bus.

The tow truck, a large one designed to haul buses and semi rigs, arrived about one hour later. The tow operator made numerous attempts to remove the bus, but was still unable to tow it out. It was now over five hours after the accident, traffic was stranded at the bottom of the road and others were screaming to get down the road.

Aside from all of the pressure from outfitters and other river users to get up and down the Cunard Road, there was another influence to "wrap it up" and open the road. At about 3:45pm and over five hours after the bus accident, we received a report from a river outfitter that had just launched from Cunard; they had "found a dead body along the New River just downstream from Cunard". The outfitter had gotten on the river late because of the volume of river traffic, so the trip leader decided to pull the group over earlier than normal and provide the picnic lunch to their customers. One of the customers had walked downstream about thirty yards and had found the body. The trip leader used his portable radio to call their base, who in turn called the NPS dispatch to make the report. The outfitter decided it was best to take their customers out of the area and not expose them any further to the body. They radioed in the general location as being one mile downriver from Cunard, and then paddled down the river.

The response to the "body found" call was delayed while we waited for the tow truck winch cables to be cleared from across the road. During the attempts to remove the bus the tow operator had moved it a few feet, allowing other buses to safely get past. So I made a decision to halt the towing operation. I had the tow operator secure the bus with blocks and chains to prevent from rolling any further, and had the tow truck moved out of the road so it could be opened to traffic. Of course we had to station a ranger on the site to direct traffic to prevent other accidents at this site. We had the tow operator return to the area on Sunday and this time he brought a second tow truck and operator. With the two trucks working together the bus was removed fairly quickly and without any further problems.

We had a raft and two rangers at the top of Cunard Road ready to do a river patrol "sweep", so after clearing the road we sent them downriver to do a hasty search for the body. I also sent two other rangers downriver on foot to search the area along the river bank in the general area. It wasn't until about 11:00pm when we finally located the badly decomposed body. It was about 1.5 miles downstream from Cunard along the river bank, one half mile further than what the outfitter had reported.

The advanced decomposition of the body indicated that it had been in this location for at least a week and had been exposed to high water from the rising river. Since it was dark we weren't going to do a very good job of processing the scene until daylight. So we left a ranger on the area overnight to protect the scene, a necessity for evidentiary purposes, and came back the following morning.

Most of the park is concurrent jurisdiction, meaning that the Feds and State share jurisdiction, so we quickly got the Fayette County Sheriff and the WV Medical Examiners Office involved in the investigation. The next day we processed the scene with the joint investigative team. It appeared that the body may have washed down from upstream and came to rest at its present location and with the washing from the river there wasn't much physical evidence left at the site of the body. About all we had to go on was the clothing on the corpse and the corpse itself. So, it was up the WV Medical Examiners Office to give us some leads to work with. The Medical Examiners Office determined that the body was a black male and had been dead approximately two to three weeks before he was found on the riverbank. Nothing was conclusive at the time, and even though it could have been an accidental death, there was evidence obtained in the autopsy that gave us cause to believe that it could have also been a homicide. So, we treated it as a homicide, and placed in it in the hands of the park's Special Agent for follow-up investigation. I won't give the punch line away at this time, but will say that when the investigation was concluded about a year later this one turned out to be material for a dime store mystery novel – but then, that's another story.

While we were dealing with the "body" call, we received another emergency report. This time it was in the Arbuckle Creek area of the park, about five miles upstream from Cunard. Acting as the overall Incident Commander for the park I knew that it was time to "triage calls". A woman had fallen off of a horse and taken a six foot fall causing head injury and lacerations around her eyes. She had fallen from the horse onto the trail, so there was not any technical rope rescue involved. Since we had other major incidents going on, and because we didn't have anyone that could break away and get to the area in time to help, I decided that we had to let the local Fire Dept. and EMS providers handle this incident. A private EMS company was dispatched to the area along with the local VFD. After the victim was stabilized at the scene she was evacuated about one half mile out the trail by an ATV to the waiting ambulance. The ambulance transported her to a helicopter landing zone where she was loaded into a medical helicopter and flown to Charleston, WV for emergency treatment. She was treated for a concussion, glass was removed from her eyes from her broken eyeglasses, and she was released on Sunday.

While we were dealing with these three incidents we received another emergency call. The report was a domestic violence incident at the Stonecliff Beach Camping Area near Thurmond. Rangers arrived and found one of the persons involved had left the area and the incident was now defused. The rangers interviewed two intoxicated women at the campsite. From the interview with the women and other campers the rangers determined that a local man, his niece and sister were drinking heavily all day around the campsite. They had gotten into a loud argument that eventually broke into an all out brawl between the man and two women. There were bruises and abrasions on the women's face and arms that they said were made by the man during the fight. It was a typical domestic violence case that was all too familiar to the rangers in that area; the rangers would try to locate the man in a follow-up investigation. Assault and disorderly conduct charges were pending on the conclusion of the investigation.

While rangers were dealing with the disorderly conduct at Stonecliff another complaint was received at the Gauley Tailwaters Campground on the Gauley River NRA. The report was for disorderly conduct and larceny. Two rangers arrived and found the campers in a heated argument. In order to sort things out and to get a clear picture of what had occurred they had to separate the campers. After getting things calmed down the story finally began to come into focus. As it worked out it was another all night drinking party in the campground; campers from the two sites were involved in the "partying" all night when things went sour. An argument started over something, but now no one really remembered what it was, and escalated into a pushing, shoving, rolling on the ground, and punch throwing fracas. One of the persons "violated" in the assault huffed off and allegedly came back later and stole some camping gear from the other camp. No one was hurt in the incident except a couple of scraped and bruised egos. The rangers, doing their part as good moderators cited both parties with disorderly conduct and evicted them from the campground. The larceny could not be confirmed at the time, that would take some follow-up investigation.

On Saturday afternoon rangers were called to a motor vehicle accident on Royal Road near Grandview Sandbar. They found that the car had been traveling at a high rate of speed on the narrow, windy road. It had missed a curve, left the road, and rolled over a fifteen foot high embankment. The car was a total wreck, but somehow the three young men in the car walked away without any injuries. The driver was cited for reckless driving. A wrecker was called to pull the car back on the road and tow it away, and the rangers found rides for the three persons involved in the wreck before clearing the incident.

While other rangers were inundated with the incidents that were happening on Saturday we had another planned "event" that was taking place. Our river patrol rangers were dealing with another "special event". The Northeast Regional Director was scheduled to visit the park on the Saturday of Memorial Weekend, and our river patrol rangers were going to take her downriver from Cunard to Fayette Station, a six and one half mile trip through class 4+ whitewater. After weeks of planning to make sure the park looked its best, and that we had everything in place, the Director arrived. The river patrol with the Director and her party launched from Cunard, while we were dealing with the bus accident at the top of the Cunard Road. I guess it's a good thing that we had planned it well enough for her to be past the road block caused by the accident; at least it hadn't interfered with her river trip.

Honestly though, there was a lot of planning that went into the trip and the preparation for the visit by every division in the entire park. This was the person that the park superintendent reported directly to, and the person that held the purse strings for all the parks in the region. Impressions are important in that political world. The important thing is she was impressed, not only by the great river trip, but by all of the, diverse, exciting, and dangerous incidents that the rangers were dealing with in such a narrow span of time. It caught her attention and did pay off later when the park applied for additional ranger staffing.

The author with Vice President Dan Quayle after accompanying him and his family down the New River, one of the numerous VIP river trips the ranger staff facilitated.

After the VIP trip concluded I had the river patrol come back to Cunard in order to launch a second trip for their normal "sweep" of the river. We ran this patrol to assist other boaters in distress, and in an attempt to make sure everyone got off the river safely. It was a good thing we had them come back to Cunard, because we were able to put them on the river immediately to search for the body that had been found downriver from Cunard.

Thankfully, Saturday came to an end without any further major incidents, at least any that we were aware of at the time. We still had the rest of the long weekend to go, and as it turned out the "storm" wasn't over yet.

On Sunday morning rangers received a report of another assault, this time at Grandview. When rangers arrived they found the reporting party was a local woman who said that on Saturday evening she had been attacked by a stranger along the Canyon Rim Trail and pushed over a steep rocky slope falling about six to eight feet. She had spent the night along the park trail, and had walked out of the woods early Sunday morning where she reported the attack at the park visitor center at Grandview. She appeared frightened and disoriented and the only physical injuries she had were some bruises, scratches, and abrasions. This time, at least at first blush, it appeared that this was not your typical domestic violence case. This was a lone female hiker that had apparently been stalked along the trail and attacked without any provocation on her part.

A search dog was brought in to help identify the attack sight. Her purse was found but little other physical evidence. We did get a sketchy description of the alleged assailant, but so far nobody matching the description had been located. This one was not going to be solved immediately; it was going to take some detective work and weeks of follow-up.

On Sunday evening rangers responded to a report of a possible drowning at Sandstone Falls. The man reporting the incident said that he had observed a man wading across the top of the waterfall; a major falls that spans the entire width of the river and averages about thirty feet high for the entire distance. He said he had watched the man walk about one hundred feet across the top and then fall off of the top and into the waterfall below, in a section that was over thirty feet high. The river was running at a high flow at the time, and any fall in the area indicated would have most likely resulted in death.

A hasty search was conducted in the dark. Boats were used to search at the base of the waterfalls and along the river bank below the falls. But this was a very dangerous operation to be conducting at night, particularly for a probable recovery and not a rescue. So the search was called off for the night and continued on Monday morning. The search continued along with interviews with the reporting party and other persons that had been in the area during the time of the alleged fall. About mid-day the reporting party started giving conflicting reports. After some time it became apparent that he had fabricated the entire story. The search operation was called off until rangers could sort this out through investigation. The search would resume later in the week if new information showed a fall had actually taken place. As it turned out, there was no need to continue the search. After a couple days of follow-up investigation it became conclusive that the man had fabricated the entire story. The man admitted that he was "just making a joke". The bottom line was he got the attention he was seeking. The Federal Magistrate gave him plenty when he later appeared in court for the "Interfering with Agency Functions" charge.

On Monday morning, while we were dealing with the reported drowning at Sandstone Falls, we received a report of a fatality from gunshot wounds in the Glade Creek area. Rangers arrived shortly after the report came in and found the victim in his vehicle located at a pull-off along the road leading to Grandview Sandbar Campground. The male victim had a fatal gunshot wound to the head. Rangers worked the case as a joint investigation with detectives from the Raleigh Co. Sheriff Office. The preliminary investigation showed that the death appeared to be self inflicted. The victim was a local man who had recently been indicted by State authorities on about forty counts of sexual assault to his daughter when she was between seven to fourteen years old. After follow-up investigation the death was ruled a suicide.

The holiday weekend was finally over, but what a ride it had been. Luckily, it's not always like this, but it can be at almost any time. The intense stress, danger, and drama that the rangers deal with can take a toll at times – it can take a week to catch up on sleep, not to mention the paperwork. It can be dangerous work, as well as physically taxing but the hardest part can be the "wearing of so many hats". One minute you're a "cop", the next the "medic", and the next a "rescue technician", and those roles can often change back and forth during the same incident - but then, I guess that's part of the lure of being a National Park Ranger.

SEARCH AND RESCUE

"...We are searchers and rescuers. It is our task to remove unfortunate persons from precarious situations, whether they be trapped high atop a lofty perch, in the icy grip of a swollen stream, or lost in a dark woods. As a whole, we demonstrate a collective group of specialized skills required to extract patients from extreme environments. From violent ocean swells to murky swamp backwaters; from the penetrating cold of high peaks to the oppressive desert heat; from wide open spaces to dense woodlands we shall go forth, often placing ourselves in the path of adverse conditions and imminent peril, that others may live.

From the 'National Ranger Code of Honor' -- by Ranger Kevin Moses

THE BUFFALO STAMPEDES

Buffalo National River in the Ozark Mountains of Arkansas is truly a beautiful National Park area. High limestone bluffs line this beautiful free-flowing river the length of the one hundred thirty five miles within the park boundaries. The park is divided into three districts, the Upper Buffalo, Middle Buffalo, and Lower Buffalo. Each district has its own unique character, its own draw to the public, and its own set of issues and problems.

The Buffalo River flows west to east in more or less the middle of the State of Arkansas. The Upper Buffalo District begins in the western end at the headwaters and runs downstream to Hasty, a distance of over 37 river miles. The Upper District also includes about 35,000 acres, several caves, six campgrounds, miles of high bluffs or cliffs and about thirty five miles of park roads. During the 1980's the district ranger staff consisted of the District Supervisory Ranger and three permanent field Rangers. In the spring and summer the staff was supplemented by one Seasonal Ranger and a park volunteer if the budget permitted.

The section of river on the Upper District comprises most of the whitewater in the park consisting of class I, II, and III rapids (using the International Grading System for whitewater, Class I is the easiest with gentle rapids or ripples, and Class VI is the most difficult and dangerous). Because the river is free flowing the water level is dependent on rainfall. The more rain the higher the river – higher generally means more technical and difficult for most river users. The vast majority of boating on the Upper District is canoeing with most of it coming from rental livery outfitters, therefore most of the canoeist are inexperienced or novice.

The spring of the year generally brings the highest rainfall period of the year, therefore making it very popular with whitewater thrill seekers, and of course very popular with the college spring break crowd. Hundreds of boaters descend on the 8 mile river section of river between Steel Creek and Kyles Landing. The unwritten rule seems to be that most of the boaters are inexperienced and/or have an over abundance of alcohol along on the trip.

My job as the Steel Creek Sub-district Ranger was to manage all visitor and resource protection activities within the sub-district, an area that ran from the western boundary of the park to Kyles Landing, a distance of 16.7 river miles, and about 18,000 acres. The Sub-district area also included the Ponca Wilderness Area, Boxley Valley, Lost Valley Campground, Steel Creek Campground and a shared responsibility for Kyles Landing Campground. My protection duties included Law Enforcement, Search and Rescue, Emergency Medical Services, Firefighting, and "others duties as assigned", in other words whatever came up was mine. This is a large area with lots of duties and lots going on, and with the exception of one park volunteer that helped me with the Lost Valley Campground during the spring I was what you might call the "Lone Ranger".

Saturday April 30, 1983 was a very busy day at the Steel Creek boat landing. Outfitters were having a banner day. Hundreds of canoes were being launched at the landing site that morning. The weather was cold and raining, and after spending the day managing the crowd at the launch area it was apparent to me that this was going to be a very busy day on the river so I began to prepare for a river patrol. It had rained all night and the river level was up and was continuing to rise. It was going to be one of those days - I could feel it in my bones.

George, my campground volunteer, is a very good canoeist and occasionally would come along with me on a patrol. I called him and said "Hey George, looks like its going to be a big day on the river, want to come along?" Of course George was always looking for an excuse to get on the river said "you bet, I'll grab my gear and meet you in thirty minutes". It's never a good idea, even for an experienced river runner, to boat alone; and since my gut was telling me this was really going to be a busy day on the river I was glad to have George along. George was not only a good canoeist but was a member of the park Search and Rescue Team and had good EMS skills. In short he was good hand, and a good person to have in your corner. George was what we call in the service a "wanna be" ranger, and a couple years later he did attend a Seasonal Law Enforcement Academy and became a Seasonal Park Ranger.

We launched our patrol from Steel Creek in two separate canoes; we were hardly around the first bend from the launch when we ran into the first problem. A group of four canoeists were on shore of a small island below a class II rapid yelling for help. It was obvious to us what the problem was, but we pulled over and asked "What's the problem?" The two men and two women were all soaking wet and shivering and one answered "We dumped our canoes in the rapid and lost all of our gear". I noticed that one canoe was pulled up on the downstream end of the island but the other canoe was nowhere in sight. They had also lost all of their paddles and other gear. Since it was obvious they were in the early stages of hypothermia we gathered up a pile of wood. I reached in my dry box and pulled out a long red tube and walked toward the fire. One of the men asked "you going to blow us up with a stick of dynamite"? "No", I said "I'm going to get a fire started and get you warmed up". What I pulled out of the box was of course not a stick of dynamite but a simple road flare. It's a trade secret, if you want to get a fire going fast, even when your firewood is soaking wet use a road flare, they work like magic. Within five minutes we had a good blaze going and the group was getting warmed up. Now that their brains were warmed up they could think and make some critical decisions. Once warmed up they asked "What should we do now, one canoe and all of our paddles are gone, how are we going to get out of here"? I replied "Well, you have two choices; we can round up your canoe and paddles and continue downriver, or you can walk back upriver about three hundred or four hundred yards to where you put-in at Steel Creek". The group talked it over and decided "Our car is at the takeout at Kyles Landing, if you can get our gear we want to continue downriver". It just so happened that other canoeist had grabbed their lost canoe and pulled it over to the right side of the river about one hundred yards down river. George and I rounded up the canoe; the paddles were also inside the canoe so we didn't have to do any more searching. We got the gear back upriver to them and left them there to contemplate their decision. As we explained to them they had a long way to go downstream, they were wet and cold and if they hiked a short way back upriver they could hitch a ride with an outfitter to Kyles. The canoes and other gear could be retrieved later by the outfitters. It was their decision, I'm not sure which way they ultimately decided but since we didn't see them anywhere downriver later I think they made the right decision.

We left the group there and George and I continued downriver. We weren't very far downriver when we ran into the next problem just below another Class II rapid and on a bend in the river. The river was really up and swift at this point. The class two's were quickly becoming more than most of the boaters could handle. This next rapid was a repeat of the same scenario we had just left, this time on the right shore. It was larger group this time, all wet and cold and suffering from mild hypothermia. We pulled over and I told them to start gathering up wood for a fire. I pitched them a flare and asked "you know how to use a flare"? "Yeah" one of the guys shouted. I told them to get the fire started close to the river on that gravel bar, to get warm and stoke the fire before you leave to keep it going. "You won't have to worry about the fire getting away in this rain. There are other people coming behind you that will probably need it" I told them. I truly wasn't worried about the fire getting away because the rain was coming down in a steady drizzle. Hypothermia is a real killer and I was more worried about saving lives from the cold than a fire getting started at this point.

As we continued downriver, the scene was a continuation of the river "carnage" we had seen just upriver. The river was rising rapidly; most of the canoeist had limited boating skills and were having a real tough time handling the water conditions. Luckily I had a whole ammo box stuffed with about 20 flares. We didn't have time to stop and get a fire going for everyone so we would pull up, give them instructions on getting a fire started, tell them to leave it going after they left, pitch them a flare and continued downriver. By this time we had about ten "saves" and we weren't downriver more than two miles from our launch area. We had a long way to go, the water was rising, and I knew it was going to get worse before it got better.

We stopped at Hemmed-in-Hollow, about four and one half miles downriver from the launch area to eat lunch before continuing downriver. The river takes a sharp right hand bend at this point and is normally a tricky area for most novice canoeist, even at lower water levels. With the river continuing to rise, the run was becoming very challenging for even an advanced canoeist. Because of the potential for problems at this particular location it had become an area where we routinely set up to assist and sometimes rescue canoeists in trouble. On this particular day it was utter mayhem, needless to say we never got a chance to eat lunch. No sooner did we sit down on the river bank than we were pulling boaters out of the water. After about fifteen minutes on the site we had already had another ten rescues, most by throwbag or by wading out in knee deep water to grab someone or their boat before they were swept downriver into the strainers. We were about ready to leave and continue downriver when IT happened. Two guys in a canoe came downriver around the bend, "gunwale grabbing", totally out of control, and a look of utter fear on their faces. They lost it right in the bend just upriver from where we were sitting. Their canoe tipped over with one person flushing out and frantically swimming toward the river left shore. I jumped up and ran into the water and grabbed him just before he was swept downriver into a strainer of willows, and pulled him to shore. Behind me the boat continued downriver with the other canoeist holding tight to the boat. Unfortunately he was on the downstream side of the boat, not a place you want to be. Within an instance the boat was swept into the willows, pinning the canoeist between the canoe and the trees. The inside of the canoe was facing upstream and it immediately filled with water, trapping his legs between the boat and the trees. A sixteen foot canoe holds about five hundred gallons of water; at 8.3 pounds per gallon, he had over 4,100 pounds of weight from the water in the canoe alone. Add in the pressure from the force of the current and now the total weight or pressure on the canoeist legs is probably well over three tons; needless to say he was in agony and screaming at the top of his lungs. The harder he tried to pull his legs out, the more the canoe rolled, pulling him down into the river.

I dropped the first person on shore and turned and ran toward this second victim, dove in and swam to the canoe. I was barely able to reach the boat without being swept downriver myself. After reaching the boat I tried to roll the bottom upriver, attempting to empty it while moving it off of the victim. I was not able to roll the canoe, but was able to get on the inside of the boat and hold the victims head up out of the water. George threw me a rope, and while holding the victim up with one hand I tied a rope to the boat gunwale with the other. George rallied several other boaters that had just arrived on shore and put them on the end of the rope while I held onto the victim and also attempted to rock the boat and help roll it. After several attempts we were able to roll the canoe over, emptying it at the same time. The canoe popped up out of the river, and the victim pulled away from my grasp and was swept downriver. I jumped away from the boat and swam after him (narrowly missing getting pinned between the boat and the trees myself). I reached him in the swift current just as he was being swept into another strainer, and was able to wrestle him out of the grasp of the willows. He was semi-conscious when I reached the shore with him.

On shore we brought him around to full consciousness, actually he mostly did this on his own as a result of the pain he was in. A medical assessment concluded that he had an angulated fracture of his ankle and a possible dislocated knee in the other leg from where he had been pinned between the canoe and willows. The patient was lying on the ground moaning in pain, George was gathering up materials to make a makeshift splint for his ankle and leg, and I was at the head of the patient trying to calm him. Other boaters were beginning to gather around to see if they could help. All of a sudden this lone kayaker, still wearing his spray skirt, his helmet and a nose clip walked up and squatted down at the patients' feet, he grabbed and lifted the patients' foot and announced loudly to no one in particular "I know First Aid, can I help"? Well the patient let out this death curdling scream and the kayaker dropped his foot back to the ground, naturally causing another death curdling scream from the patient. I jumped up and confronted the kayaker, telling him to back off and leave the treatment to me. Believe it or not he still didn't get it, and insisted on helping with the treatment. After I threatened to arrest him (and maybe even with bodily harm) he finally got the picture and backed off.

Senator Dale Bumpers (Arkansas) offering his congratulations after the author was awarded the Department of Interior Valor Award.

After the episode with the kayaker George and I immobilized the patients' foot and knee using spare paddles, sticks, padding from the first aid kit, extra straps, and of course duct tape that I carried with me just for this type of purpose. With his legs immobilized it was time to transport him to the takeout at Kyles Landing, about three and one half miles downriver. Since we were in a wilderness setting the only way to get him out was to canoe him downriver. Bystanders helped us load him into my canoe and with the patient lying in the bottom of the canoe I began to paddle him downriver. Luckily the river was no longer rising from the rain earlier in the morning. Even though it was still tricky in spots it wasn't as treacherous as it had been and I was able to get him safely downriver without further incident.

At Kyles Landing there was an ambulance waiting to transport him to the hospital in Harrison, AR, about thirty five miles away. He was treated for a fractured ankle and a badly sprained knee. He was released after a couple of days in the hospital and was expected to make a full recovery. The last time I saw him was when we placed him in the ambulance. He thanked me for helping him and asked me if I got the name and address of the kayaker so he could properly thank him as well!

Incidents of this nature were considered by most of the ranger staff as a fairly typical early spring day on the river. There's plenty of excitement and lots of challenges. I was pretty used to the dangerous nature of my job, "hanging it over the edge" as we put it; so I didn't think that I had really done anything out of the ordinary during this particular incident. In fact, I have personally been on several other incidents before and after this incident that were more demanding and had a greater potential for harm to myself than this one. However, somebody was apparently impressed with what took place and did a good job of keeping it a secret because it was over a year later before I was notified by my supervisor that he had nominated me for and I had been approved to receive the Department of Interior Valor Award – the highest Valor Award in the U.S. Department of Interior. Almost two years after the incident took place; on April 25, 1985 I attended a Dept. of Interior Awards Ceremony in Washington, DC and received the U.S. DOI Valor Award from the Secretary of Interior for "heroism above and beyond the call of duty, while risking life to save another".

COLD STUFF

Newfound Gap Road is the most popular scenic drive in the Great Smoky Mountains National Park. Beginning in Gatlinburg, TN at an elevation of 1340 feet, it climbs to the top of the gap which sits on the TN/NC state lines at an elevation of 5,048 feet, it then descends the other side of the mountain into Cherokee, NC at an elevation of 1988 feet. This elevation change of over three thousand vertical feet makes for some of the most scenic and breathtaking views in the park, and of course it also makes for major changes in temperature and weather conditions, especially during the winter.

During the summer months you can expect the temperature at the top of the mountain to be as much as ten degrees cooler than the temperature in the foothills at the bottom of the mountain. During the winter these temperature and climatic conditions are dramatically different, you may be experiencing a balmy day at the bottom of the mountain while the top of the mountain is having a major winter snow or ice storm.

Since the Great Smoky Mountains National Park is an International Biosphere Preserve the environmental concerns and restrictions are understandably very stringent, therefore salt or other chemicals cannot be used on the roadways to help melt ice and snow. The park road maintenance crews do an exceptional job of plowing and sanding the road, but without the use of salt or chemicals snow quickly can change to ice, and the ice can stay on the road for days or even weeks at a time.

Weather conditions on the mountain can change very quickly, and with the change in weather the road conditions deteriorate very rapidly. Even during normal weather conditions the road is very steep and winding but when extreme weather hits the area the road conditions can be extremely hazardous. During the winter months the park ranger staff closely monitors the weather and road conditions to determine if there is a need for the road maintenance crews to respond with snow plows and sand trucks. The road is kept open as long as possible, especially during the daytime periods, but once the ranger staff determines driving conditions are too hazardous the road is closed. The gates are closed on either side of the mountain, and rangers "sweep" the road to make sure everyone gets off the mountain safely. Unfortunately, the park does not have the funding or personnel to allow rangers to staff the park twenty four hours a day, and there are times when winter storms strike after the ranger staff has gone off duty for the evening.

Such was the case on November 18, 2002, a cold wintry day. It had been cold but dry all day and the forecast was calling for the temperature to drop into the low teens overnight but no precipitation was called for. As has been proven many times in the past, the predicted weather is not always accurate. After the ranger staff went off duty that evening a sudden winter storm hit the mountain dumping about four inches of snow at the higher elevations; almost as soon as the snow hit it turned the road into a sheet of ice.

A motorist left Cherokee and headed north on a dry road and by the time he hit Newfound Gap the snowstorm hit. He stopped at Newfound Gap to assess the road conditions but quickly determined that he needed to get off the mountain before the conditions worsened. Not sure whether he should turn back toward Cherokee to the south or continue north toward Gatlinburg, he chose the latter and started very slowly down the mountain on the steep and winding Tennessee side. The road was slick and treacherous but he was able to continue down at a very slow pace. When the motorist thought he had made it past the worst sections he increased speed and continued down the mountain. This, however, proved to be a mistake since the road was still solid ice. In the vicinity of the Chimney Top Trailhead, and just above the "Loop" (a 360 degree turn in the road), his car spun out of control on the snow and ice covered road, went off the roadway and plunged over the steep embankment. The car rolled down a twenty foot embankment, continued down the steep slope another thirty feet and finally came to rest upside down in the icy waters of the West Prong of the Pigeon River.

Traffic accident on the Foothills Parkway Spur in Great Smoky Mountains National Park. Accidents such as this one are a frequent occurrence on park roads and often end up over steep embankments and in rivers, and creeks.

Even though the driver was seriously injured, he was able to finally free himself from the vehicle and crawl into the icy river. However he was not able to pull himself all of the way out of the water and he remained in the icy waters for over forty minutes before help arrived. Luckily, shortly after the vehicle skidded over the side, another motorist noticed the skid marks on the road leading over the embankment and stopped to check it out. Looking down the embankment from the road the motorist was able to see the vehicle upside down in the river below. He stopped another motorist and had the driver go for help while he stayed in the area to see if he could locate any injured persons. Cellular telephone service is almost non-existent along Newfound Gap Road, this area was a complete dead zone, so the motorist had to drive about ten miles down the mountain to the Sugarlands Visitor Center area before he got cell coverage and was able to call 9-1-1 to report the accident.

The 9-1-1 dispatcher called the National Park Dispatch immediately. Rangers from the Tennessee and North Carolina Districts were immediately dispatched to the accident. When the first Ranger arrived on the scene along Newfound Gap Road where the vehicle went over the embankment he was met by a very excited man stating that he could see the car overturned in the river. It just so happened that the first Ranger on the scene was also a Park Medic. He grabbed his medical bag and started down the steep slope toward the overturned vehicle. Initially, in trying to locate a path to the victim his route took him to a vertical cliff that blocked his passage. After looking around for a few minutes he was able to find a steep but accessible route over the embankment to the streambed and the overturned car. When he reached the vehicle the ranger/medic searched but did not find any victims inside. It was dark at the time and not knowing if the occupants were thrown from the vehicle and lay injured nearby, or if they had "walked away" from the accident made the search of the immediate area much more difficult. He continued to search the area and call out for the occupants. After searching for a couple of minutes he found the patient about thirty feet downriver, the lower two thirds of his body was still in the river. The patient was severely injured and he was in the advanced stages of hypothermia. He was only semi-conscious but was able to relay, with some difficulty, to the ranger/medic that he was in the car by himself when it plunged over the hillside. The ranger/medic immediately pulled the patient out of the river and began medical treatment. By this time the motorist had been in the water for almost an hour. The medical assessment showed that the patient, aside from

34

being extremely hypothermic, had a six-inch laceration on his head, a fractured clavicle, and several fractured ribs.

The ranger/medic began the job of stabilizing the patient, and administering advanced life support. Other rangers arrived about fifteen minutes later along with the Gatlinburg Rescue Squad. The patient was treated for the life threatening injuries on site, stabilized and packaged in a Stokes litter for transport up the steep slope and vertical cliff to a waiting ambulance.

In order to get the patient up to the ambulance rangers had to utilize their technical rescue skills. A technical litter raise was utilized that allowed them to get the patient up the embankment and the vertical wall to the roadway in about twenty minutes. The patient was loaded in the ambulance and transported to Gatlinburg Fire Department where they were met by a LifeStar Medical Helicopter. He was flown to the University of Tennessee Medical Center by air ambulance, and was admitted into the neurological intensive care unit in critical condition. After over a week in intensive care the patient was released to his doctor's care and was expected to make a full recovery.

The quick response, excellent emergency medical care, use of excellent rescue skills, the questioning of the patient and other witnesses at the scene, and overall professional care and treatment from everyone involved undoubtedly saved this victims life.

In looking back at the incident, even though the patient was conscious and coherent through most of the treatment by the ranger/medic, questioning and getting information from the patient to determine what his injuries were and if there were other passengers in the vehicle was difficult. But the communications did work – this was in spite of the fact that the patient was a foreign national and SPOKE ONLY CHINESE!

FROSTBITE – A NEAR DEATH EXPERIENCE

On Wednesday December 21st, 2005 at about 4 p.m. the Sevier County 911 Center received a broken cell phone call. The only words from the caller that the dispatcher was able to make out before the call was dropped were "Appalachian Trail", "frostbite", and "fall". Since the caller sounded like he was in distress and probably in the park, the 911 Center called the Park Dispatch Center and relayed the message to them.

The park was in the middle of a winter snowstorm and temperatures were bitterly cold, so this call precipitated a series of phone calls to rangers throughout the park. Off duty Rangers were directed to report back to duty and gear up for a major search and rescue operation.

Once the initial group of rangers arrived at Park Headquarters we began to analyze the information we had and formulate a plan. However, at that time the only information we had was the cell phone call itself, with only the three identifiable words – "Appalachian Trail", "frostbite", and "fall". Repeated attempts to re-contact the person by the cell phone were unsuccessful, forcing us to make some assumptions. The choices we had to consider were: 1) it was a prank call, 2) the caller's phone was out of range, 3) the person was unable to answer the call, or 4) the phone battery was dead.

Fortunately the 911 Center had recently upgraded their dispatch equipment, so they were able to give us the number of the cell phone. From that we were able to get the name of the person listed to the phone. The phone was listed to a sixty-two year old Knoxville, TN man. I have chosen to call him Daniel Trailblazer for this true account. After receiving information on his name, we were able to get his home phone number through cross-referencing, thereby allowing us to try to call his home. Our hope was to reach him or someone there who could give us information that would help in the case. Unfortunately, all we got at his home number was a telephone recorder. After more than an hour of working the telephone, mostly calling neighbors, we finally made contact with Mr. Trailblazer's daughter.

Meanwhile we had been cross referencing vehicle information for any vehicles owned by Mr. Trailblazer. At the same time we had information from his daughter and neighbors that Trailblazer was an avid hiker and frequently hiked in the Great Smoky Mountains. In addition, we learned that Trailblazer had planned a trip into the Smokies this week and they thought he was presently hiking somewhere in the park. We also pulled all information we had from our Backcountry Registration System, present and historical records, and there was not a backcountry permit for Trailblazer. But it did show that Trailblazer was a frequent backcountry hiker and camper in the park. After getting a description of Trailblazer's vehicle, Rangers were sent to trailheads throughout the park in an attempt to locate his vehicle. Locating his vehicle would give us a "jumping off point". As it stood right now our search area involved "the world" – obviously, we needed to narrow the area down a whole lot.

While we were working the other "leads" we also found out that the new digital radio equipment from the Sevier County 911 Center also allowed them to conduct a data triangulation on the phone call and give us the location of where the call came from. This basically meant that when a call comes into the center they have the ability to triangulate between the cellular antennas spread throughout the area and get a "fix" or location of the caller when he placed the call. This was one of the first times this system had been used by the Sevier County 911 operators, and the first time we had used it in the park, so we weren't sure how reliable it would be. The data triangulation from the 911 center allowed us to plot the coordinates, giving us a general location of where the call came from when the 911 Center received it. The coordinates indicated the caller was in the Park, and somewhere between Greenbrier and Cosby, but it also showed that the location was about three miles north of the Appalachian Trail. Since the triangulation fix showed the area to be near the Maddron Bald Trail we immediately mounted a "hasty search" of the Maddron Bald Trail and the junction of Old Settlers trail. Two Rangers were sent on this hasty search in an attempt to quickly locate Trailblazer, and if they found no sign of him we could at least rule out the area. It was about 6 p.m. when rangers began to check the trails. There was about one foot of fresh snow on the ground in that area, and there were no signs of Trailblazer, or signs that other hikers had used the trail coming up from the bottom or down from the top.

Since several trails, including the Appalachian Trail are in the area near the coordinates it was very hard to determine exactly which trails to search for Trailblazer. The weather was really lousy, the temperature was around five degrees at the time, the wind was gusting over twenty mph, and reports from Mt. LeConte were that there was about two feet of snow on the Appalachian Trail. The truth of the matter was, even if it had been perfect weather we simply didn't have enough searchers to search all of the trails in the area in time to do a hiker in distress any good. What we needed was more information to help narrow the search area.

Finally, around 9 p.m. a ranger who was checking trailheads located Trailblazer's vehicle in the Cosby Campground; now we had that "jumping off point" we had been looking for and we were finally beginning to narrow the search area down a little. While rangers were checking out the vehicle and making contact with campers in the campground to see if they had any information relating to Trailblazer, Park Dispatch received a phone call from three hikers. The hikers had just returned to their vehicle at Cosby Campground and were reporting another hiker in distress on the Appalachian Trail (AT). Rangers quickly located these hikers in the campground and learned that they had been on a backpacking trip on the AT and had just hiked down the Snake Den Ridge trail to the campground. They had seen Trailblazer on the AT and had hiked out with the intent of calling the park to get him help. The hikers told the rangers that at about 3:00 p.m. they had come across this hiker on the AT near Inadu Knob (elevation 5,918') and located about three miles directly south of the cell phone coordinates. According to the hikers the man identified himself as Daniel Trailblazer. They said he had severe frostbite, especially on his feet, was severely hypothermic, only semi-conscious when they left him, and that he had very little food, water, or camping and survival gear with him. Before leaving him they had tucked him into a sleeping bag and he was lying on a foam pad on the side of the trail. After making sure he was as warm and dry as they could make him they left Trailblazer and hiked out to Cosby to make the report.

So now we knew where he was and that his condition was poor. We began to make preparations for the rescue and evacuation. We knew there was a small helicopter landing zone (LZ) near Inadu Knob, but we also knew that the weather conditions would not permit the helicopter to be used at that elevation. We also knew that even if the weather were perfect a night evacuation was out of the question on that small LZ. If a helicopter was to be used at all it would have to be a helicopter equipped with a hoist. That activity, however, would have to wait until daylight.

So the helicopter option was out for now. That meant we had to go get him on foot, in the dark. We would send in a medical team to try to locate and stabilize him; once that was accomplished, it would take no less than fifteen trained rescuers to carry him out by litter. Considering the hikers report on Trailblazers' condition, and the worsening weather conditions we knew that speed in reaching and getting him to a hospital was going to be critical. We would go forward with the ground carryout plan for now, but would continue to work on getting the specially equipped helicopter.

A hasty team was assembled, and at about 4:00 a.m. a team of three Rangers, two EMT's and a Park Medic, began hiking to Trailblazer with the intent of locating, accessing and stabilizing him until additional personnel could arrive to assist with the carryout, or until he could be hoisted out by helicopter. It was six miles to Inadu Knob, all of it rough going. The hasty team started out in about eight inches of snow but toward the top they were in snow over two feet deep, with drifts of several feet. They reached Mr. Trailblazer at about 7:30 in the morning. They found him at Inadu Knob as indicated by the hikers, buried in a snow bank alongside the trail. He was unconscious, still in his sleeping bag, and as feared he had severe hypothermia and severe frost bite on his hands and feet. When they were finally able to arouse him it was only into a semi-conscious stupor. These three rangers, all three proven backcountry Rangers with superior wilderness skills, and one a very experienced Medic did exceptional work in warming the patient, feeding him warm liquids and bits of food to get his strength up, keeping his spirits up, and taking care of his frostbitten limbs, while all the while being in a fight with the elements for their own survival.

The author secures an injured patient in a Stokes Litter in preparation from a rough overland evacuation.

41

The rangers managing the incident had worked through the night to locate a helicopter capable of performing the task at hand, and at about 8:30 am two Tennessee National Guard helicopters, one a Blackhawk with hoist capabilities, were launched to attempt a hoist evacuation. On the top of the ridge at Inadu Knob high winds, sustained at about forty miles per hour with gust of seventy miles per hour, forced a halt to the helicopter operations after the first attempt. The helicopter was simply getting blown all over the mountain. It was impossible to make a safe hoist extrication in those conditions. The pilot later said that "the winds were so bad we were barely able to crest the top of the ridge, and as soon as we did we were blown back".

With the helicopter out of the picture we pressed forward with a ground litter evacuation team. A winter storm warning with high winds was in effect and it had begun to rain at lower elevations and spit snow at higher elevations increasing the urgency of the rescue. A team was assembled and made up of about twenty National Park and Tennessee State Park employees. This was an experienced, field hardened team. It would take the best team we could put together to accomplish this task since the elements combined with the trail conditions were extreme.

The litter carry-out team reached the victim at Inadu Knob and found the hasty team had stabilized Trailblazer. He was conscious and able to take in hot liquids. It took about twenty minutes to "package" Trailblazer in the litter, using a "mummy wrap" technique of several layers of sleeping bag, blankets and tarps to keep in the warmth and repel any snow or other moisture. The rescuers began the carryout, luckily most of it downhill from this point, alternating between carrying the litter and dragging it through the snow toboggan style where possible. The going was as rough as it gets and they had to stop on multiple occasions to check on their patient as well to check on the status of the rescue team. After several hours of carrying and dragging the litter the six miles down Snake Den Ridge Trail they finally reached the Cosby Campground at about 9:30 p.m. Trailblazer was placed in an ambulance that was waiting at the trailhead and transported to a LifeStar Medical Helicopter that was waiting at an LZ on the Foothills Parkway. From there he was flown to University of Tennessee Medical Center. At the UT Trauma Center Trailblazer was treated for hypothermia; severe frostbite of both hands, and moderate frostbite of the feet. As a result of the severe frostbite Trailblazer lost a couple of toes on both feet, but fortunately he survived with his fingers intact. The prognosis was, however, that he would probably lose some function in his fingers.

It was later determined by interviews with Trailblazer that he began his ill fated adventure on December 18th when he left his vehicle at the Cosby Campground and began a hike up the Appalachian Trail to Tricorner Knob Shelter, a distance of eleven and one half miles. During the afternoon of December 18, while in route to Tricorner Knob he lost the trail in the deep and blowing snow, slipped and fell on a steep embankment and was unable to get back to his feet after becoming entangled in his pack and tree branches. A snowstorm on December 20th dropped an additional ten inches of new snow making a total of twenty-five inches of snow on the ground. During the period from December 18th to December 21st temperatures ranged from a high of thirty-three to a low of minus fourteen degrees. Laying on the trail, Trailblazer endured frigid conditions for three and one half days before being rescued.

So what's the lesson here? First, you always need to be prepared when hiking in the wilderness, especially in the winter. Never count on the weather forecast to be exact, and always make sure you have all of the proper gear and extra food and nourishment. Second, it's never a good idea to hike alone, especially during the winter on long backpacking trips. Third, make a pre-plan of your trip, and always leave an itinerary with family or friends so help can be called if you fail to meet your agreed upon finish or check points. Fourth, if at all possible use a cell phone to call out to family or friends periodically to give them a status check. It will give them peace of mind and it may safe your life.

RESCUE - FALLING ACCIDENT
AT GROTTO FALLS

Rescue and Emergency Medicine can be very satisfying experiences for the emergency providers. However, from an emotional and psychological standpoint it can also be very difficult over a long career, or even over a busy season. Over the course of more than thirty years as a ranger I have had the opportunity to be involved in hundreds of serious accidents and incidents involving searches, rescues, emergency medical situations, wildfires, natural disasters and law enforcement responses. Many of these incidents had very successful outcomes; those are always very satisfying to be involved in. The successful ones are easy to deal with, but the ones with a negative outcome can be hard to deal with for even the most hardened emergency provider. Deaths and traumatic injuries are always tough to work, especially when a young person is involved and is left permanently impaired, or is fatally injured.

This feeling of dread is compounded even further when someone gets seriously or permanently injured by doing something totally unnecessary. There seems to be an unwritten rule that most of the serious incidents that occur in our national parks are usually caused by people not following regulations, by disregarding posted warnings, or by not following good common sense. This may seem harsh, but it is all too often the case. Some of these "rules" may apply to an incident that occurred in November 2008 when a park visitor (we'll call him Jimmy, a 25 year old Knoxville, TN resident) went on a hike with some friends to Grotto Falls in Great Smoky Mountains National Park.

It was a beautiful and balmy autumn day. Park visitors were out everywhere in the park, hiking, touring, fishing and otherwise just enjoying the day. I was heading up into the Greenbrier area on a personal photography expedition. I've spent an entire career working in parks, but I still thoroughly enjoy getting into the park just like any other visitor. I've always had an affinity for nature photography and had recently bought a new digital camera, so on this day I intended to follow one of my passions and go for a hike to photograph the waterfall on the Ramsey Cascades Trail. I didn't get that far though, as I was driving past the Greenbrier Ranger Station I saw one of my ranger buddies, who I'll call Craig, walking out of the station toward his vehicle, I decided to stop and say "hey". We chatted for a couple of minutes when Craig received a radio call from another ranger "There's an injured hiker at Grotto Falls," the ranger said. "It sounds like a bad one, sounds like the hiker took a major fall at Grotto, and has a bad head injury. We need a medic, are you available?" Craig radioed back, "Yeah, I'll be in route," then he turned to me and asked if I could help on the rescue. I said, "Sure can, I'll take my POV (privately owned vehicle) and meet you there".

Craig ran inside to get a few supplies. I got in my vehicle and took off toward Grotto Falls. Craig passed me a few minutes later since he was running with lights and siren. Within a few seconds of reaching Rt. 321 he was out of sight as he sped up the road. Even though I wanted to drive like an emergency responder I kept it at the posted speed limit and continued my response in an orderly manner. It's about fifteen miles from Greenbrier to the access trail to Grotto Falls, and to get from one place to the other we had to drive through Gatlinburg. When I got into the park again on Cherokee Orchard Road, to my dismay I got behind what seemed like every slow driver on the road that day, a whole string of them. But I remained patient, knowing I was in a personal vehicle. A Gatlinburg Rescue Squad Ambulance came up behind me just after I pulled onto Roaring Fork Motor Nature Trail. I pulled over along with the other cars in front of me to let the ambulance by, then I tucked right in behind that ambulance and allowed it to clear the way for us up to the trailhead.

I arrived at the Grotto Falls Trailhead about 30 minutes after first receiving the report. Ranger Craig had gotten there ahead of me by about fifteen minutes. He met another ranger named Robby at the trailhead; they grabbed their EMS gear and headed up the trail. When I got to the trailhead I grabbed my day pack with some extra clothing and some first aid supplies from my truck and headed up the trail; it took me about twenty five minutes to make the 1.2 mile hike uphill to Grotto Falls.

As I was hiking up the trail I passed several groups of hikers coming down. Even though I was in civilian clothes they apparently could see that I was on a "mission" by the way I was hiking because several of them wished me luck and best wishes for the patient. Of course, the more I received these comments the more it made me realize this was going to be a serious incident. When I arrived I found Rangers Craig and Robby and two bystanders working on the patient. It turned out that one of the bystanders was a paramedic on vacation from Florida and his helper was his wife. My hat went off to this dedicated couple because they had stabilized the patient until the rangers arrived and were continuing to assist. The patient was lying at the bottom of a steep cliff on a rocky ledge; luckily he was right beside the trail. The trained bystanders were stabilizing the neck and spine, allowing the rangers to get the medical equipment out of their pack to start an IV.

When the rangers arrived they found the patient lying on his back on a large pile of rocks about four feet above the trail. The fact that he had a severe head injury was obvious since he was bleeding profusely from the head. He was also semi-conscious, complained of severe pain to his head, arms and chest, and was not able to feel his legs. All he could tell the rangers was that he had slipped and fallen off the cliff near the waterfall. The golden rule in emergency medicine is if a patient has sustained a fall of over five feet you suspect head, neck and spinal injury and you should treat it as such; so all spinal precautions were taken. We ascertained that the victim had been hiking with four friends, two women and two men, and these companions said that their friend Jimmy had fallen off the cliff immediately above where he was now lying. At first glance it was apparent to the rangers that Jimmy had taken a tumbling fall of about forty vertical feet.

After falling off of the cliff top at the Grotto Falls area the falling victim is treated and stabilized by park rangers and trained bystanders.

Since the others were involved in the patient treatment when I arrived, Ranger Robby asked me to start working on the investigation. Basically this meant getting the names of companions and witnesses, and witness statements to find out exactly what happened. I took down the names and contact information of his four companions, and from them I found out that the two men with Jimmy had hiked up to the waterfall from the left side. They took an old unofficial "social" trail that leads up around a rock outcropping and climbs to the top of the cliff. The path is more of a steep walk up and around the rock outcropping and does not require any technical climbing skills. The young men then walked along the top of the cliff and over to the right toward the waterfall. While at the waterfall they took some photographs, and after a few minutes Jimmy joined them. Jimmy had not taken the same route to the waterfall as his two companions; he had started up from the right side of the waterfall and climbed up a rough boulder strewn path trail and had come up to his friends from the opposite side of the creek. They all took a few minutes admiring the waterfall and taking photos. Then Jimmy started back down by himself, taking the route that his friends had taken to the top. Jimmy had a head start of about one minute on his friends and was out in front of the group by about one hundred feet. Because of the vegetation between Jimmy and his friends, they had lost sight of him on the trail ahead. When Jimmy's friends came up to the waterfall they followed a beaten down path which stayed away from the edge of the cliff; since Jimmy did not come up this way he apparently missed the obvious path and walked toward the cliff looking for the route down. He was standing right at the top of the cliff near a standing dead tree looking for a route down when his two friends heard him yell. From about 50 feet away they saw him slip and fall over the edge of the cliff. His frantic friends then ran over to the cliff edge and to their horror saw Jimmy lying at the bottom of the cliff. They yelled down to their companions at the bottom, and were told that Jimmy was seriously injured. They ran back to the path they had taken up to the waterfall and were able to get to the bottom safely.

The witnesses at the bottom of the cliff saw Jimmy walk to the cliff edge, heard him yell and looked up and saw him slip off the edge of the cliff. The cliff that Jimmy had fallen from was directly above where he was now lying, and from the description of the fall it was very apparent that he had taken a horrible fall of about forty feet from a nearly vertical cliff. Nearly vertical means that he probably tumbled down the cliff and struck protruding rocks in several places during his descent before he reached his rocky landing point. The injuries to his head, arms, chest, and legs also made it evident that it was a very nasty tumbling fall and that he struck the rock cliff in several places on the way down.

Before starting my hike up to Grotto Falls I had also grabbed my camera and stuck it in my pack. I used it now to document the accident site, taking several photos of the cliff, the falling site, the patient landing position. It had rained the day before and the trail and wooded area around the trail were wet and muddy. The turf at the top of the cliff sloped downhill to the bare rock directly on the edge, and from the slide marks at the top of the cliff it was apparent that Jimmy had gotten too close and his feet had simply slipped on the wet soil and he slid directly over the cliff edge.

In addition to the friends Jimmy was hiking with that day, there were several other hikers at the falls when he fell, and these good folks sprang into action. The first persons to reach him stopped the flow of blood from his head wound and kept him immobile, two qualified emergency medical providers went to work immobilizing and treating him for shock, several others offered their assistance in helping to treat him, others got out cell phones and began calling for help, and others started down the trail to get help in case the phone calls were not successful. After several attempts one of the bystanders was able to dial 911 on their cellular phone. Sevier County 911 received the call and in turn called Park Dispatch, and the rapid response was started.

With the rangers on scene and the IV going ranger Craig called Park Dispatch on his two-way radio and had them relay critical information about the injured party to medical control at University of Tennessee Trauma Center. From the "med control" trauma doctor ranger Craig received permission to administer pain-killing and other medicines intravenously. In emergency medicine, particularly in a wilderness setting, we rely mainly on a rapid response, stabilization of the injuries and rapid transport to a medical facility. These three elements are critical to the patient outcome during what is known by emergency providers as the "Golden Hour". The main elements of emergency stabilization are immobilize, treat for shock, treat pain, and administer oxygen. Within a couple of minutes of arriving on scene all these items had been accomplished except for administering oxygen; somehow the wrench for the oxygen tank had gotten lost or left behind. The rangers tried everything to open the tank but to no avail; they needed a wrench or tool of some type to open the valve. Unfortunately no one had a Leatherman or similar tool, and scissors or other tools available would not work. After thinking about it for a few seconds I pulled out my trusty "el-cheapo" Bass Pro folding knife (I say "el-cheapo" because I got it free as a door prize on a visit to Bass Pro). I asked ranger Craig to hand me the oxygen tank. In looking at it I knew that the knife blade wasn't going to do any good, but the handle had two slotted holes that narrowed at each end. I placed the handle slot on the tank valve, jammed the narrow end onto the valve stem and twisted; "presto," the tank valve opened. As a matter of fact it worked like it was intended to be a valve wrench; we hooked up the tank and mask and got the oxygen started on Jimmy. Later we used the knife "wrench" several more times while switching out oxygen tanks on the carry out, another proof positive that the Ranger Credo "Improvise, Adapt, and Overcome" really does work (actually I think Clint Eastwood said this in the movie Heartbreak Ridge, but it applies to Rangers of all types - so I've decided to steal the phrase!).

Before I got to the injury scene and as I was hiking up the trail from the trailhead parking area I had heard another siren entering the trailhead parking area; this would have been the Search and Rescue truck. It was loaded with lots of other useful gear. It also had the litter and part of the litter haul team. There's a lot of equipment that has to be brought up to the rescue site on a litter evacuation in the backcountry. Part of the equipment is the litter, which is a strong and rugged basket in which we can strap in the patient. At the Smokies we also use a wheeled "Teton Litter" that has a single motorcycle wheel supported by an aluminum frame with a bicycle type handlebar with a hand brake on the rear, along with a step through "rickshaw" type handle on the front. Along with the basket litter and wheeled litter, the litter haul team also brings up rigid and inflatable backboards, head immobilization blocks, blankets, sleeping bags, tarps, extra clothing for the patient, extra oxygen tanks, and other medical supplies. With all the needed gear piled inside the litter it generally takes about six rescuers to haul the litter up to where the patient is located; more staff are needed as the distance and steepness increases. As soon as the haul team arrived at the trailhead all of the equipment was thrown into the litter and the litter team began the quick run up the mountain pulling over one hundred pounds of gear.

It took about forty minutes for the litter haul team to arrive at the accident scene with the litter and all of the equipment to begin the job of stabilizing and "packaging" the patient for a long ride out to the trailhead. First we placed a full body inflatable splint on the backboard, and then we placed him on a long rigid backboard. We then inflated the traction splint to further immobilize and help pad him for the ride out, and then covered him with several layers of blankets and a sleeping bag to keep him warm. Finally we wrapped him in a plastic tarp and strapped him securely into the litter. We then strapped the litter onto the wheeled Teton Litter. Patients who are in shock usually loose body heat rapidly and we have found that with an injured and immobile patient the risk of hypothermia is very high, even during warm weather. It was cool this day, in the forties, so extra care was taken to make sure the patient had plenty of warm layers. The wheeled litter supports the patient in the basket litter and allows two rescuers (one in front and one in back), to guide and haul the litter for short distances on narrow portions of the trail. For most of the journey we also used at least two additional litter attendants on each side of the litter to help support and carry the litter over rough terrain. The wheeled litter is a lot easier than carrying the litter, but even with the wheel it's still a lot of hard backbreaking work. Believe me when I say the wheel helps. I started in the rescue business when wheeled litters were not widely used, and have done a number of rescues where we had to carry the patient overland in a Stokes litter without the help of a wheel; the wheel is a godsend, but there is still a lot of hard work involved. In this transport we had to carry the patient 1.2 miles out to the trailhead over very rugged terrain. Luckily most of it was downhill. Even with the wheeled litter, because of the numerous rocks and roots in the trail the litter had to be lifted for much of the trip. This was a very rough ride for the patient, but Jimmy was a trooper and handled it with grace. He remained alert the whole way down to the trailhead, he never complained and kept his spirits up the whole way down. The litter transport down to the trailhead took about one hour; we reached it without further incident.

After the arrival of the litter haul team the patient is "packaged" for an overland litter transport to the trailhead and the waiting ambulance.

The Motor Nature Trail is a one way road, and when the last ranger that was coming into the incident entered the road he closed and locked the entrance gate behind them to keep additional traffic from entering. It was therefore decided that the ambulance would exit the area going out the wrong way toward the entrance at Cherokee Orchard. A LifeStar Medical Helicopter was standing by at the landing zone at Gatlinburg Fire Department. The Gatlinburg Ambulance arrived at the LZ about twenty minutes after leaving the trailhead and Jimmy was transferred to the helicopter for a twenty minute flight to University of Tennessee Trauma Center in Knoxville.

At UT Trauma Center the initial assessment of Jimmy's injuries was that he had sustained a fractured skull, crushed vertebrate, severe spinal injury, fractured leg and had blood in his lungs from broken ribs.

Three weeks after the accident Jimmy was still in the hospital. He was placed in a medically induced coma and placed on a ventilator for over two weeks to help fight the head injury, fight infection, and improve his breathing. After three weeks in the hospital his doctors determined that he did not have a severed spine and did not have brain damage like first thought. He did have a severe lung infection, but his high fever was now back to normal. His pneumonia was also beginning to clear up and he was off the ventilator.

After three weeks in the intensive care unit Jimmy had come out of the coma and the doctors thought he was responding positively, although they also knew that he was still fighting for his life. On December 3rd, just a little over three weeks after entering the hospital he slipped back into a coma and died a couple of days later. The massive infection sustained by the severe injuries from the fall proved too much for him to be able to recover.

The patient, his family, his friends, and yes even the emergency responders and the hospital medical team had gone through a lot of pain and anguish, but this sad event could have been avoided. Please heed this warning and learn from this tragic accident, STAY ON THE TRAILS, especially in areas like waterfalls. The water fall areas in the parks are posted with warning signs for a good reason; these areas are rocky and very slick. We have learned from past incidents that visitors get seriously injured when they go off trail and attempt to climb around on the rocks and cliffs in these steep and slippery areas. An accident can happen to anyone, and it only takes a second to slip and fall. As Jimmy and his family and friends tragically found out, making this mistake can change your life in an instant. Please learn from this tragic example and don't make these same mistakes. Use good judgment, obey the posted signs, and obey the rules. Doing so will help you stay healthy.

SURF'S UP – A SWIFTWATER RESCUE

The Great Smoky Mountains National Park has something to offer for everyone, over half a million beautiful acres, over 900 miles of hiking trails, over 384 miles of scenic roadways, wildlife galore, numerous historic buildings, and over 2,115 miles of uncontrolled streams. The latter are a godsend to fisherman and other outdoor enthusiasts, but because they are not controlled by any type of impoundments they can become a real problem after a major rainstorm. When storms drop a large amount of rainfall in the upper reaches of the drainage the walls of these steep mountain canyons act as a funnel, bringing large amounts of water into the streams and swelling them rapidly. Often, there may be a major rain event occurring in the upper elevations of a drainage, and the lower elevations of the same drainage are not receiving any rain at all. In these cases there is little or no warning of the stream rising. Fishermen and anyone else on, in or near the river may be taken by surprise when the river sudden rises.

Such was the case on the afternoon of June 22, 2004 when a family was having a picnic at the Chimneys Picnic Area. The Chimneys Picnic Area is located about 2.5 miles up the Newfound Gap Road from Sugarlands, and is positioned right along the West Prong of the Little Pigeon River. The river in this area is about two hundred fifty feet wide, is strewn with huge boulders and at lower water levels is calm and a favorite of trout fishers and others who like to explore the river. However, at higher water levels the boulders create a major whitewater stream that is used by only a handful of half crazed expert kayakers. These extreme boaters are better known within the river running community as "steep creekers" or "hair boaters".

At about 5:30 pm four brothers and sisters between the ages of 8 and 14 years old were with their parents in the Chimneys Picnic Area. The family was enjoying a picnic and the four kids were having fun wading and exploring the river near their picnic site. While their parents were preparing their picnic lunch and relaxing around the site the four kids continued playing along the river bank. In an attempt to reach the other side of the river, all four children rock-hopped out into the river, which is about two hundred fifty feet wide at this point. There was a very light rain shower falling in the picnic area at the time, but it didn't seem to be a threat to parents or the kids at this point. However, unknown to the kids and their parents a major thunderstorm was passing through the area and had already hit the drainage upstream, between Newfound Gap and in the Road Prong stream off of Clingmans Dome Road. As the kids rock-hopped across the river it began to rise at an alarming rate, and because they were closer to the opposite side of the river at that point they continued to move that way away from the picnic area side. Even with the river rising around them and covering many of the rocks that had been dry only moments before, all four of the children were able to reach a large boulder near the middle of the river. They were a little over halfway out into the river at this point, and about one hundred fifty feet from the river left shore where their parents were. Within a few minutes the river had risen four to five feet from the time they started their rock hopping journey to the opposite shore.

The kids were trapped in the middle of the river with a flash flood raging down on them. The thunderstorm was caused by a cold front rapidly moving into and colliding with the warm front over the area. With the cold front moving in and dominating the low pressure the temperature had also dropped almost ten degrees. The rain had picked up and was now a downpour so not only were the kids trapped on a rock in the middle of the river with whitewater all around them, the river was rising rapidly and threatening to sweep them off the rock and into the raging river. They were also wet, cold, and terrified, and in grave danger.

When their father heard the screams from his children, he ran to the river and began to hop across on boulders toward them shouting instructions for them to stay where they were on the large boulder. He was on a boulder about thirty feet from the river left shore when he realized that the river had risen to a level that prohibited him from reaching the children. In fact, once he turned around he realized that the river had risen higher behind him and he now couldn't return to shore either. He was trapped on the boulder about thirty feet from shore and was also in danger of being swept downriver in the swift current. He was now stranded on his own little "island" and was just barely within shouting distance of his children.

A park maintenance worker was working in the picnic area at the time and noticed the river rising rapidly. From his knowledge of the area he knew that it was a flash flood so he started around the picnic area warning visitors of the possibility of a flash flood and to stay away from the river. As he was giving his warning to picnickers along the river a visitor told him the four children were stranded on the rock in the rising river. Without wasting any time he grabbed his two way radio and contacted Park Dispatch to report the emergency.

As soon as the call went out from Park Dispatch rangers from the Sugarlands area immediately responded. Anticipating the need for help, rangers from other areas in the park dropped what they were doing and also began to move toward Chimneys Picnic Area. As the Tennessee District Ranger I assumed the role of Incident Commander for the incident and called for all available rangers and SAR Team personnel to respond to the Chimney Picnic Area with Rescue One. Rescue One is a dedicated rescue vehicle that is fully equipped for rope, river, and backcountry rescue. It contained all the equipment we would need to conduct a technical river rescue, including an inflatable boat. Rescue One was also stationed in the Sugarlands area, about three miles away so the response would be quick. I also had dispatch contact the Gatlinburg Fire and Rescue Dept. The park has a mutual aid agreement with all of the fire and rescue squads surrounding the park. In this case the Gatlinburg squad was the closest to the Chimneys. They also participated in training with the Park SAR Team and would therefore be a major asset as the rescue progressed.

A swiftwater rescue of four persons stranded in the middle of West Prong of Pigeon River in (Great Smoky Mountains NP) in August 2001 using a highline pickoff technique. The victims were stranded in the river by a flash flood in the same location as described in "Surf's Up" story. (Photo courtesy of the National Park Service)

I arrived at the Chimney Picnic Area about twenty minutes after the initial call. As soon as I got there I radioed dispatch with a size-up of the situation saying, "we have four children stranded in the middle of the river, all four are on a large boulder in the middle of the river, the river is at flood stage and is rising rapidly, the victims are completely stranded and in danger of being swept off the rock and into the river. There is also a man, I think the children's father, who is also stranded on a boulder in the river about thirty feet from shore. I think we can reach the man with a boat, I need Rescue One here ASAP". Since their father had been shouting to the children to stay on the rock, they were all huddled together and were supporting each other, so at the moment they were relatively safe.

Since the father was only about thirty feet from shore and within relatively easy reach I made the decision to attempt his rescue first. Rescue One is equipped with an inflatable raft, life jackets (PFD's), helmets and all the needed river rescue gear, as well as the necessary ropes and hardware to affect almost any type of technical rescue. Two rangers pulled up with Rescue One just a couple of minutes after my arrival. We quickly got the inflatable raft down off the top of Rescue One and inflated it. The water was really up, and at this level the huge boulders in the river bed created very technical and dangerous whitewater. At flood stage this section of the river is considered a class V - VI run by kayakers, so we didn't want anyone, even in an inflatable raft to get swept downriver. Practicing the "KISS" or "Keep it Simple" principle of swiftwater rescue, we decided the best and safest approach to reaching the father was to try to reach him without putting a rescuer in jeopardy. We shouted to him what we intended to do, he agreed and we got started. After making sure he knew not to attempt to jump in the river once he had hold of our rescue rope, we threw him a rope, he was able to catch the end on the first attempt. We then attached a PFD to our end of the rope and had him pull it in and put it on himself. We then attached his rope to the bow of the boat, attached a second rope to the bow that we kept on the shore, and attached a third rope to the stern of the boat. He pulled the boat toward his boulder and with the two ropes on the shore side we were able to guide it to him. Once he had the boat up to the boulder he was able to step into the boat. We then guided the boat into an eddy below the rapid and safely into shore without any problems. From start to finish the maneuver had only taken about ten minutes to safely pull off. We now had one person rescued, and four to go.

While we were working to get the father safely to shore we were also working on several different plans that we could use to safely affect the rescue of the four children. By this time the Gatlinburg Fire/Rescue Dept. had arrived on the scene, so we had the extra help we needed. In river rescue incidents we always to try to go with the easiest and safest techniques first, basically using the REACH, THROW, ROW, GO –

59

TOW, HELO method of rescue. We knew they were too far from shore to Reach or Throw something to them, we MIGHT be able to Row to them, HELO or Helicopter was out of the question because of the tight forest canopy along the river. We MIGHT be able to reach them by "GOing" to them, with wading as potentially the safest option and swimming to them as the last resort.

In the rescue business it's never a good idea to "put all your eggs in one basket", so after some discussion we came up with three alternatives. ROW was going to be our first attempt; we were going to try to reach them by boat. At the same time we were sending four rangers to the river right side, this would allow us to attempt to reach them by wading if we were not able to get to them by boat. As a last resort we could try to reach them by setting up a highline across the river and conducting a "Tyrolean" rescue.

Rangers practice a swiftwater rescue pickoff from a highline at the Sinks on Little River in the Great Smoky Mountains NP. Several deaths and serious accidents have occurred at this site so periodic training sessions are conducted here involving the park SAR team and outside emergency response agencies. (Photo courtesy of the National Park Service)

Luckily we didn't have to boat, wade or swim anyone across the river to get rescuers to the other side. There was a bridge on Newfound Gap Road just downriver about three hundred yards from our present location; we could send personnel to the other side by having them walk across the bridge. They could then walk upstream along the river bank, and through the rhododendron hell, about three hundred yards until they were directly across the river from us. Because they had to pick their way foot by foot through the "Rhodie Hell" it was going to take at least thirty minutes for them to reach the location of where the children were, and directly across from us.

Because of the time it would take to get the rescuers to the other side we went ahead and put into play option one – try to reach them by boat. The river at this location was a very steep boulder filled gradient, and as mentioned, at flood stage is considered to be class V+ whitewater. That meant that this boat rescue attempt was going to be very tricky, there was no room for error. Rain had now stopped in the immediate area, but a spot weather forecast indicated that additional thunderstorms were expected in the area within an hour. We knew that additional rainfall would continue to raise the river creating a greater threat that the children would be swept downriver; this increased the urgency of reaching them NOW. We were also fighting time, since at this point we only had about two hours of daylight left.

The swift current and the huge boulder strewn river bed created four to five foot drops in the river upstream of us, so it was not possible for us to put in upstream and use the rivers currents to sweep downriver and across the river to where the children were. As an alternative we decided to put in almost directly across from where the children were. This was a tricky maneuver; we didn't want to get swept downstream in this intense water so as a precaution we tethered ropes to the bow and stern of the boat. That way we would have help from the shore in case we were swept down and away from the children. The most experienced boaters jumped in the boat, which happened to be a firefighter/medic from Gatlinburg Fire Dept., and a ranger. The boat team made two attempts at paddling over to the children, but each time they were swept downstream in the swift current. Luckily, we had attached the tether to the boat and the shore tenders were able to pull them back to shore before they were swept too far downstream and into the intense whitewater below.

By the time the boat was pulled back to shore after the second attempt we got a radio call from the six Rangers that had been sent across the river. They had made it to their destination, and were now directly across from us on the river right shore. From their position the river right group were able to see the children, and were able to communicate with them by shouting; this had a very positive affect on the children who up to this point felt like they were doomed. The river was beginning to drop a little and the rain had stopped. The rangers thought that they could make it to the children by wading out to them as a group. So the six person rescue team, anchored by "Big D", a mountain of a ranger at six foot and seven inches tall and weighting in at three hundred pounds, started out toward the children using a multi-person wading technique. Using a human chain and assisted by a safety rope to help stabilize them in the chest high whitewater the wading team was able to slowly work their way out to the children. One by one they brought the children back from their rock perch in the middle of the river to the safety of the river right shore.

The children were wet, cold and frightened but otherwise all were in good shape. The rangers warmed the four children as best they could by sharing the extra dry clothing they had with them. They then walked the children out along the riverbank and the heavy undergrowth of the rhodie hell, reaching Newfound Gap Road about forty minutes later. There was a joyous reunion with their parents back in the picnic area, and a big round of applause by all of the picnickers that had gathered around to watch.

This was a very close call, but the outcome was excellent; no one hurt and WHAT AN ADVENTURE to talk about in school next fall. Whatever the outdoor activity you are involved in always know the weather forecast, keep your children close and closely supervise them, and remember, when you're around moving water things can change in a hurry.

BATTERIES NOT INCLUDED

Every park has certain trails and backcountry areas where there is an inordinate amount of visitor use; unfortunately, because of the heavy volume of visitor activity these areas usually have a large volume in incidents. Great Smoky Mountains National Park has several of these areas.

Everyone that visits the Smokies wants to do some hiking, but most visitors don't have the equipment, expertise, or the time to spend the entire day in the backcountry, or a multi-day backpacking trip. So Laurel Falls Trail is one of those "frontcountry" trails that gives an alternative for the entire family, a quick day hike of about one and one half miles on a paved trail. The hike uphill to the upper and lower waterfalls and back to the parking lot generally takes about two to three hours. But the downside is, since it is so accessible and the prize at the end is a beautiful waterfall, this trail is extremely crowded.

Of course, with all of these visitors you're bound to have some injuries. Luckily, most of the accidents are moderate and involve sprained, twisted, or broken ankles. Over the past several years there have also been several serious injuries from falls of twenty to thirty feet. In fact, at one point between 1998 and 2001 the park was having such a rash of accidents involving fractured ankles and legs rangers were having to do carryouts from the area an average of eight times per month. When I transferred to the Smokies in January of 2002 one of my first tasks, in addition to my normal duties as District Ranger, was to research the accidents that had occurred at Laurel Falls to find out what was causing them, and what we could do to reduce or prevent them.

When I researched the incident reports I found out that most of the accidents were ankle and leg injuries that occurred on or near a small footbridge that crosses the creek between the two main waterfalls. I found that the concrete footbridge stepped off onto a humped rock on the creek side. When hikers stepped off the bridge onto the uneven rocks it caused them to roll their ankles, causing the injuries. In addition, when you stepped off of the bridge onto the creek side you were standing on top of one of the thirty foot high waterfalls. This area is uneven and slippery with a very real potential for the visitors in this area to take a very nasty thirty foot fall to the bottom of the waterfall. There also were no warning signs or physical barriers that would prevent or reduce the falling hazard at this location. After identifying the problems I wrote up my findings and presented them to the park management team. Basically it was pretty simple, smooth out the landing zone on the end of the bridge, and do something to get the word out to the public that standing on the edge of the waterfall was hazardous to their health. The management team agreed on my findings so the plan then went to the park maintenance division to put into action. In working with maintenance on a solution it was decided that the best and most permanent way to solve the problem was to simply cut the top off the rock at the end of the bridge to level it. With that accomplished we then decided on signs along the edge of the waterfall that warned the public of the danger, as well as additional signs that would warn against climbing on the waterfalls. All of this seems pretty simple and maybe even overkill, especially the signage. You'd think people would use good common sense and figure this out for themselves, most do, but others seem to have to see it in writing. The bottom line is - **it worked**; after the renovation was completed the accidents dropped of dramatically.

However, with the volume of traffic to this location, and the rugged nature of the area some accidents did continue to occur but at a much reduced rate. As it stands today, during the busy visitor season from May to November the park gets an average of about two accidents resulting in treatment, litter carryout, and follow-up medical visits per month.

Since the trail is partially paved to the waterfalls and only moderately strenuous it gets use from just about everybody. All experience levels and visitors with various physical abilities from the physically fit to couch potatoes. I've seen quite a few baby strollers, and wheel chairs going up the trail. It's tough on the pushers, but doable, and even with the crowds everyone seems to enjoy the short hike to the falls.

But as mentioned before, accidents do continue to occur on the trail, and rangers do continue to respond and do carryouts. I have personally been on over twenty carryouts on the trail, most resulting in a quick run up the trail with a litter, packaging the victim in a wheeled litter and a carryout down the trailhead to a waiting ambulance. There were some that involved much more technical equipment and expertise, and some that required a bit more ingenuity – perhaps even a sense of humor.

One incident in particular that required ingenuity and a sense of humor occurred in the summer of 2006. Even though it was only mid-afternoon, it was a fairly busy day in the park. Rangers had already responded to several traffic accidents, bear jams, campground complaints, and normal traffic control and enforcement work. At about 2:00 pm park dispatch received a call from the county 911 center, a visitor had called in by cell phone saying that a wheel chair bound man was down on the Laurel Falls Trail up near the waterfall. There were no details on the nature of the "injury" so a hasty team of two rangers headed up the trail on foot with medical equipment to assess the nature of the problem. They would radio additional information back to a litter team that was coming up behind them. When the first two rangers arrived they found a man that weighed over six hundred pounds on a battery powered scooter designed for the disabled at the footbridge leading to the waterfall. The man was not injured but had numerous medical problems, and the battery on the scooter he had ridden the one and one half miles up the trail was completely dead; he wasn't going anywhere on it. He was stuck, he had to get down the trail to take his medicine and he was in a panic.

The hasty team rangers radioed the info back to the litter team that was headed for the trail that they would need additional help to get the man in the litter, and with the carryout downhill to the parking lot.

Dispatch put the word out to all park divisions for assistance, and within minutes there were about ten additional responders coming to assist with the carryout. The litter arrived with two additional rangers but the four rangers, even with assistance from bystanders, were unable to lift the man onto the litter. When the additional help arrived they were able to lift him, but they quickly found out that he was too large for the litter. The container was simply too small for the contents. This called for some thought, it was decided that they would bring a "gator" up to the scene to try to move him. No, not an alligator, a gator is a six wheel ATV with a small dump bed on the rear. The plan was they would load him in the dump bed of the gator and use it to haul him out to the trailhead. They also asked for an extra battery to try to jump start the scooter. If that didn't work they would use the gator to carry him down the trail.

Rangers loading up ATV Gators and Mules for a backcountry operation, the ATV's pictured are similar to the one used in the "Batteries Not Included" story. (Photo courtesy of the National Park Service)

The gator, with the extra battery and jumper cables, arrived at the trailhead about fifteen minutes later and started up the trail. The gator is a fairly wide machine, but most of the trail was wide enough to get through without too much of a problem, except for the last section of trail before the waterfall. In fact, there was no way they were going to get the gator any closer to the waterfall, where the "victim" was located than about one hundred yards. The battery and cables were connected to the scooter, but to no avail, the scooter battery was "deader than a post". It simply wasn't going to start. They would have to carry the man to the gator (it was later determined that the battery wasn't dead after all, the motor was simply fried, burned out, kaput). Well, one hundred yards is a whole lot better than the one and one half miles they were facing before, so the team set out of the first leg of their mission - the one hundred yard carry. Seems simple huh? Well, not so simple, remember, this was a really large and heavy guy, and it was already determined that he wasn't going to fit in the litter. So again ingenuity comes into play. They sent someone back to the trailhead to pick up another backboard. When the second backboard arrived on scene they tied the two together and used them and every available rescuer - and every ounce of strength they collectively had to push, pull, and carry the man the one hundred yards up the trail to the waiting gator.

This was a steep uphill section going back out, and it took over thirty minutes to go that one hundred yards, but they finally reached the gator. "Now", they thought, "we're making progress". Again, not quite that easy; using all the strength the team could muster they lifted him up and put him on the bed of the gator. When he was lowered into the bed the front wheels of the gator lifted up off of the ground from the immense weight, and the tailgate buried in the ground. On the second attempt they decided to lower the dump bed down, slide him into the bed and slowly lower the bed. To compensate for the weight they had to load four rescuers on the front "fenders" of the gator. Finally they had him secured in the bed of the gator, but they would have to ease down the trail with the driver, passenger, and two others on the fenders to compensate for the weight in the bed. Despite the concern for the brakes holding the load going downhill and driving very slowly down the trail the rescue team finally made it the one and one half miles to the trailhead without any further problems. When they reached the trailhead the man was reunited with his family. After the rangers made a quick trip back up the trail to "rescue" his scooter he was on his way. Another successful rescue accomplished.

So, can you see the morale of the story here? Now I proudly admit that I don't need to, nor have I ever driven one of those scooters, so I personally don't know if they come with a warning about where you can and cannot take them. But common sense should dictate that even a normal sized person, let alone a six hundred pound person, would at least think twice before riding one of these devices one and one half miles uphill on a mountain trail. So I guess the morale of the story is: make sure your battery is fully charged before going off on a "hike" - right?

THE PIT AND THE
MOUNTAIN CUR

There are a few areas within the National Park System, like National Preserves, National Rivers and National Recreation Areas where hunting is allowed, but for the most part hunting is prohibited in most other NPS areas, particularly in National Parks. But that doesn't mean that hunting, or more accurately, poaching doesn't occur in National Parks. In fact, the Ranger Force was historically created in the parks as "game keepers", beginning in the big western parks like Yellowstone and Yosemite. To this day, poaching continues in National Parks, and the protection of the wildlife and natural features continues to be a major emphasis of the park protection programs even today.

Wherever you go in the U.S., hunters in different areas of the country have their favorite species and techniques in the pursuit of game animals. In the Appalachians for example, using hunting dogs to track and tree game is a favorite hunting technique. And to go a step further, within different areas the Appalachians hunters favor different game animals while using hunting dogs. The favored species tends to reflect the availability of the game in these areas, for instance, raccoon or "coon" hunting is the big sport in some areas. In other areas using dogs to run deer into the open for hunters to "take" is popular. In the southern Appalachians, around the Blue Ridge Parkway and Great

Smoky Mountains National Park, the use of dogs to hunt black bear is very popular, particularly with local hunters. In fact, using dogs to hunt black bear has been a tradition in the Smokies since the area was first settled in the early 1800's. And since the creation of the National Park in 1934 bear hunting has continued to take place along the fringes and sometimes within the boundaries of the Great Smoky Mountains National Park.

I think it's fair to say that the vast majority of hunters are honest folks; they try to follow the rules and regulations. But just as in society in general there is a small percentage of people that seem to go out of their way to go against the rules – to those few it is a way of life. Those few are the ones that give hunting a bad name; they are also the ones that rangers and other game protectors' target – believe me when I say that it can become a big "game" between the rangers and the poachers. In the history of the Smokies there have been a number of significant poaching cases that occurred inside the National Park over its 75 year history. And because of some of these past poaching activities, there has been an adversarial relationship between rangers and bear hunters that dates back to the beginning of the park.

Today bear hunting with dogs continues to be a very popular sport, and with modern technology the dogs are now typically equipped with radio collars. Since the radio collars have GPS tracking capability it allows the hunters to track the dogs through the chase, and to pinpoint their location when the bear is "treed". Once the bear is treed the hunters then go to the location and "take" the bear. The idea of GPS devices on dogs doesn't sit very well with many citizens or game protectors, so the controversy continues. When a dog is set off on a bear track or scent just outside the park boundaries, it's inevitable that dogs will sometimes chase a bear into the park. If this happens the hunter is supposed to contact the park, and let the rangers know that their dog is inside the park and is on the trail of a bear or may have one treed. The hunters are then allowed to enter the park without their firearms and attempt to retrieve their dogs. Of course this is a nuisance for the rangers because of the time commitment of "chaperoning" the hunters while on park property and the fact that many rangers feel the hunters are in violation because their hunting dogs are harassing wildlife. On the other hand, hunters use the argument that they were "hunting legally" before the dogs entered the park, and "the dogs can't read the boundary signs".

So this is an ongoing controversy, one that may never be resolved. But I have learned over a long time of working with the public that using tact and diplomacy to gain compliance usually works better than taking a hard bureaucratic stance. In 2002 when I transferred to the Smokies as the District Ranger, I was invited to the Gatlinburg Chapter of the local Bear Hunters Club to attend a meeting and discuss rules and regulations of dogs in the park, what they can do as an organization to help them stay within the guidelines, and in general how they can develop a better relationship with the park. Apparently this offer to meet had been made to other rangers in my position in the past but the offer was never accepted, because the club president who called was shocked when I accepted to the offer to attend. The members were even more shocked when I showed up and talked to the group of over fifty hunters. The meeting was tense at times, but very informative for both sides, and the benefit was that it tended to break the ice between the two groups. If nothing else a dialog was started that would help to resolve problems and the controversy between hunters and game protectors in the park. My hope was that by opening the dialog we could recruit the hunters to help police their own activity. As it turned out, it did work, even though there continued to be some episodes of bear dogs crossing over into the park. We did get better compliance from the hunters as a whole in working within the park regulations and guidelines. I continued to attend the annual bear hunters meetings; this gave me contact with the officers of the bear hunters club who had influence with the other hunters. It also gave me a place to start with if we had issues that needed to be discussed and resolved concerning bear hunting and hunting dog activity inside the park.

Believe me when I say that you can't change the world overnight, especially when it involves attitudes and feelings that have been deeply ingrained over generations. There was still a good bit of mistrust on both sides of the hunting issue, but at least we were moving in the right direction. The benefits from this new found relationship paid off on November 16, 2006, when park dispatch received a report of a dog that was trapped in the bottom of a deep natural cave on the western side of the park near Cades Cove. Rangers were sent to the area to investigate and they met with a group that had been camping in a backcountry campsite #4 off of Ace Gap Trail. The campers said that during the night they heard the continued barking of a dog that sounded like it was several hundred yards to the west of them. The barking was persistent, so after listening to it for a couple of hours they decided to grab their head lights and strike out in the dark to investigate. They hiked through the woods for about three hundred yards, the barking continued to get louder the further west they went and at one point it sounded like they were right on top of it, but they just couldn't locate it. After about forty five minutes of stumbling through the dark woods they finally came to a sunken bowl shaped area that went steeply downhill about fifty feet lower than the surrounding terrain. Shining their lights into the bowl they decided that the dog must be down in that area, but they also decided that the climb downhill into the bottom was too dangerous for them to do in the dark. They went back to camp, got a couple hours of sleep and came back early in the morning. The barking was still coming from the area so there was no problem locating the spot again. Reaching the area they climbed downhill to the bottom of the bowl. Getting into the bottom of the bowl area wasn't a problem in the daylight, but when they reached the bottom of the bowl it dropped off into a hole that was about thirty feet in diameter and about fifty feet straight down; it was a good thing they hadn't tried it in the dark the night before! Looking down into the sinkhole, actually a cave opening with a vertical shaft, they couldn't actually see the dog, but from the barking knew that he was down in the deep pit. The dog was trapped in the bottom of the sinkhole and apparently had no way out. The campers knew they didn't have the equipment or skills to get into the sinkhole to retrieve the dog, so they went looking for help. Just a couple hundred yards away they came upon a house that was under construction; there they found a local builder and asked for his help. The builder took a rope and went to the sinkhole with the campers; using the rope attached to his seat harness the builder was able to get close enough to the edge and see the dog in the bottom of the sinkhole about fifty feet straight down, but the builder was not able to get down to the dog. That evening, apparently after he was finished with his work day, the builder called park dispatch to report the incident and asked the park for assistance in getting the dog out of the sinkhole. Two rangers agreed to meet with the builder, when the rangers arrived at the sinkhole it was dark, and they could not hear any barking coming from the sinkhole. Since there was no barking or other indication that the dog was still in the sinkhole, they decided that it would be best to wait until daylight to explore the sinkhole any further.

The author at the top of the sinkhole after bringing the cur dog up from the bottom of the pit. The dog is still hooked up to the haul rope and is handling the experience very calmly.

I was called early the next morning and asked to come to the area and bring rope rescue equipment. I met three other rangers and we set off for the sinkhole; to get there we had to come in from outside the park from a sub-division near the Townsend area. The sinkhole was about one hundred yards inside the wood line, but we quickly found out that it was also about one hundred yards outside of the park boundary. Even though this wasn't our responsibility we continued on toward the sinkhole. It was very steep and slippery down to the edge of the pit, so I put on a rescue harness and set up a rappel rope. I rappelled down to the edge of the pit and looked down, as described to us it was a straight vertical drop of about fifty feet to the bottom. Standing on the edge of the pit I did not hear any barking or other sounds and looking down into the pit I didn't see any sign of the dog. Given the recent report from several two different groups, that was a bit of a mystery. Looking over the area in the bottom of the pit I could also see what could have been another small opening off to the side, maybe the dog had crawled back into a small gap in the rocks and was sleeping. The only way to tell for sure was to go down into the bottom. I was elected as the one that was going into the sinkhole. I didn't have a personal ascending system with me, so before I rappelled down I was going to set up a system to help the rangers on top haul me back out of the sinkhole. I climbed back up to the top with the other rangers and we set up a 3:1 mechanical advantage haul system. That done I rappelled down into the bottom of the pit. In the bottom I found evidence that the dog had been there but no sign of where he was now, and no sign of how he could have gotten out of the fifty foot deep sinkhole by himself. I looked around, and off to the side I saw another small opening, just big enough for me to squeeze into. I crawled over the small opening and shined my headlight into it, sure enough, this was another pit and straight down about forty feet I could see a small blond colored dog. When I called down to him he stood up and looked up at me with very sad eyes. The dog looked emaciated and wasn't moving much so he was probably hurt. He had apparently given up on help from humans and decided to try to find his own way out. During the night he must have crawled into the opening and taken his second drop of about forty feet. That's two vertical drops totaling about ninety feet, if he wasn't seriously injured it was a miracle. I threw the haul rope down into the pit and rappelled in after it. When I got to the dog I examined him, he appeared to very weak but there were no signs of broken bones, bleeding or obvious serious internal injury, it was a miracle. Another miracle, the cave continued down even further but on an angle and not a direct vertical drop. This cave may go for miles and there were probably several more vertical drops, so it was a good thing that the dog had stopped where he did. The next thing I noticed was the radio collar around his neck, no doubt a bear or maybe a coon dog that was lost during a hunt. He was a cute little guy, actually a medium size dog, but he was so thin his ribs were showing so he looked smaller than he actually was. He just melted in my hands, basically giving himself to me to do whatever I needed to do, so I used a piece of nylon webbing to fashion a dog rescue harness around. I then switched myself over from the rappel rope to the haul system and attached my new friend to my harness. I radioed to the rangers above that I was ready to go up, and started climbing while being assisted by the haul rope system. About ten minutes later, after much grunting and groaning while squeezing through the tight opening, the dog and I were back on the top. My little friend, who looked like a Cur was great the whole way up, not a peep out of him. Away from the edge I disconnected myself and my new partner, the Cur, and gave him some water which he gladly accepted. While examining the dog further we found that the dog was emaciated, exhausted, and sore but other than that he appeared to be in pretty good shape.

Back at our vehicles I fed him some snacks and an MRE (Meals Ready to Eat - prepackaged meals originally developed for the military) that I keep in the vehicle for emergency incidents; he didn't turn any of it down. Now that we had the dog out and safe we needed to figure out what to do with him. Since there was no doubt that he was a hunting dog, and most likely a bear dog I decided to call my contact with the bear club, I had his number in my cell phone address book so gave him a ring. He answered right away; he was actually on a bear hunt in Eastern North Carolina at the time, but he gladly took the information I gave him on the dog and the location and said he would make some calls and get back to me. True to his word about fifteen minutes later he called back and gave me the name and phone number of a bear hunter who had been hunting in that general area about a week ago and had lost his dog. I called the number and got a local man from the Townsend area and told him about finding the dog in the cave, he ecstatically exclaimed, "that's my dog, I'll be right there".

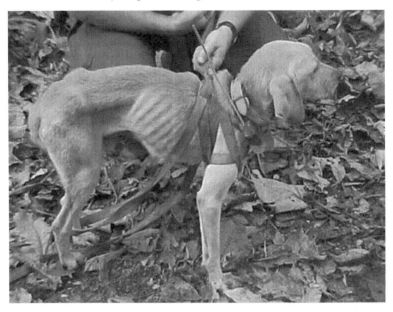

The emaciated "Pit" the Mountain Cur still in the makeshift webbing harness I fashioned around him to haul him up from the bottom of the sinkhole. The dog had probably been in the sinkhole without food or water since he had gone missing 16 days earlier.

The hunter arrived about forty minutes later, sure enough it was his dog. He said that he had been hunting the in area 16 days ago, saying "I looked for over two weeks for him; it was like he just dropped off he face of the earth. I had him on the telemetry device and all of a sudden he was gone, there was no signal". Well, that's essentially what happened; actually he dropped into the earth. It is unknown how long the dog was trapped in the cave, but by the looks of the emaciated animal it's fair to say that he was in that pit for a good part of the sixteen days. No food and maybe a little condensed moisture that he could lick off the rock ledge. I asked the owner what breed of dog he was, he said he was a Mountain Cur, proud that my thinking was right, I just smiled. Many uninformed folks use the name Cur as a form of ridicule, meaning low or worthless, but in reality Mountain Curs are the original pioneer dogs of the southern Appalachian Mountains. They were used by the pioneers to hunt bear and just about any animal that could be "treed", and are still prized by Appalachian hunters to this day. I can certainly say one thing for them, they're survivors! I heard back from the owner a week later, the dog I had affectionately named "Pit" the Mountain Cur had been treated by a vet, he was doing well and was expected to fully recover from his ordeal.

From my standpoint, what I learned from this was that you never know what kind of positive things will come from simply trying to do the right thing. Opening up lines of communication with an opposing group to try to resolve issues was the first step; the second step was going beyond expectations in rescuing a dog that wasn't even within our jurisdiction, and a hunting dog at that. The fact that rangers would go so far to help out a bear dog really had a profound influence on the local bear hunting community, the feedback was very positive from the community in general as well as the bear hunting community. The local press also picked up the story and put a very positive spin on it, I guess that also helped get the word out about the incident. Apparently that's also where the PETA (People for Ethical Treatment of Animals) heard about the rescue. About three weeks after the incident I received a very nice letter from this organization along with a certificate of appreciation, and a box of "goodies". The goodie box contained all types of vegetable based foods, the popcorn was good – but I personally don't recommend the all veggie "jerky".

TRAGEDY AT HEMMED IN HOLLOW

Buffalo River in north central Arkansas is a free flowing river; the headwaters begin in the Ozark National Forest and flow into the Buffalo National River. Under the management of the National Park Service, the Buffalo National River begins just upstream of Boxley Valley and runs east across north central Arkansas for one hundred thirty five miles, ending at the confluence of White River. The Buffalo is noted for its scenic beauty and has some of the most pristine river landscapes in the Midwestern U.S., including streams, caves, waterfalls and scenic mountains.

The area also has excellent hiking with many of the trails leading to scenic wonders; these beautiful areas are very popular with park visitors. One of the major scenic hikes in the park is Hemmed-In-Hollow. Located in the Ponca Wilderness Area, Hemmed-In-Hollow is at the head of the small canyon with cliffs over two hundred feet high and a waterfall that is two hundred and nine feet tall. The waterfall is known as the tallest waterfall between the Rockies and the Appalachian Mountains.

On a beautiful spring day in 1984 I was serving as the Steel Creek Sub-district Ranger at Buffalo National River. At about 2:00 pm while I was on patrol in the Boxley Valley, I received a radio call from park dispatch with a report of a falling accident at Hemmed-In-Hollow. Let me tell you, getting a call like this is never a pleasant feeling – your stomach just drops, your heart starts racing and your mind goes in a thousand different directions trying to think of everything you need to do at once. The person that had called park dispatch had been at the scene of the accident, and in order to notify dispatch he had run down the trail about four miles to the mouth of the river, then canoed downriver three and a half miles to Kyles Landing, and then jumped in his vehicle and drove to the nearest telephone about three miles away. It had taken him over two hours to get out to a telephone to make the emergency call. According to the reporting party, a young man had fallen about sixty feet from a cliff, and he appeared to have a head injury, multiple fractures, and maybe internal injuries – in other words this was shaping up to be a bad one.

I was about eight miles from the Steel Creek Ranger Station at the time of the report so I "ran code" and arrived at the station about twenty minutes later; not an easy feat considering the narrow, winding, steep roads in the area. I had a seasonal ranger working with me in the sub-district that had been hired just for the summer season. I'll just call him ranger George. I called George and asked him to meet me at Steel Creek. Other rangers from the Upper District, as well as the rest of the park were also responding, but the next closest ranger besides George and I was over one and a half hours away from Steel Creek.

At Steel Creek I loaded my trusty "steed", a J-10 Jeep pickup truck, with a sixteen foot Blue Hole Canoe, a rescue litter with all the technical rope rescue gear already prepackaged, and headed the two hundred yards to the Steel Creek Launch Area. At the launch area I threw the boat off and loaded the litter and other rescue gear in the boat, which added about one hundred pounds of weight. The extra weight and bulk makes it difficult for one paddler on this section of river so I strapped everything in the canoe securely while waiting for my partner to arrive.

Within a few minutes of my reaching the launch area George arrived and we were on the river paddling downriver. The river trip from Steel Creek to the mouth of Hemmed-In-Hollow is about five miles through class I - III whitewater; we pushed it hard and luckily didn't have any problems on the trip downriver. We reached the mouth of Hemmed-In-Hollow about forty five minutes after putting on the water. We loaded all of the rescue gear in the litter and headed up the trail to the waterfall, about three and one half miles up the trail. We had only gotten about a half mile up the trail when we met a group coming down toward the river carrying the injured person in a makeshift litter.

We found out that the leader of the group was a trauma doctor who worked in the emergency room of a major Little Rock hospital. The doctor and his family had canoed downriver from Steel Creek earlier in the day. They pulled their canoes up on the bank at the mouth of Hemmed-In-Hollow and hiked up the trail to the waterfall. At the waterfall there was another group with six teenagers, and one of them, a young man about nineteen years old began free climbing up the face of the waterfall without any rope or other safety devices. The man had gotten about seventy to eighty feet up the face of the waterfall and appeared to be stuck, unable to go up or down. He was trying to climb down when he slipped and fell, landing on the sharp boulders at the base of the waterfall. The doctor saw the fall and immediately ran to the fallen man, assessed his injuries and began to organize a rescue effort with the other members of the victims' party, his family, and other bystanders. First, he examined the patient and found that he had a very severe head injury, possible neck and spinal fracture, multiple fractures of the arms and legs, and possible fractured ribs, chest, and internal injuries. Second, he instructed someone to run out to make a call for help, knowing that the response by any emergency providers would be a long way off. Third, the doctor began to treat the patient; he used clothing from himself and other persons present to fashion improvised splints, a cervical collar to immobilize the neck, and stabilize the spine as much as possible with the "tools" at hand.

Park Rangers treat a "patient" during a high angle rescue training course. Routine training like this help rangers sharpen their patient assessment, stabilization, and other EMS skills, as well as their technical rescue skills.

The patient was in and out of consciousness for the first few minutes; he then lost consciousness completely and was having trouble breathing. The doctor knew the only way to save this young man was to get him out to advanced medical help, so after stabilizing him as much as possible he decided to begin transport out to the river. He supervised the others on the scene to build a makeshift litter out of jackets and poles and clothing from the other persons on the scene. Then he and the other members of the victim's party and other hikers began to slowly carry him out the three and one half miles to the river.

After we met with the victim and his rescue party and interviewed the doctor and examined the injured party, we decided it would be best to place a real cervical collar on the patient, transfer him to the long spine board and litter which we had brought up with us, and get him out to the river for transport downriver as soon as possible. With the doctor's help the transfer only took a few minutes, and we had him at the river's edge in about thirty minutes after the transfer. Now in 1984 medical helicopter life flights out of the backcountry of Buffalo River was not an option. So the only options we had were carryout by litter or canoe downriver to the nearest launch area. I knew I had other rangers responding to the area who could help in an overland carryout, but I also knew that they were over one hour away. I also knew that a carryout from this point to Kyles Landing, about four miles downriver, would take over four hours; and that clock wouldn't start ticking until the other rangers arrived. The doctor said the patient's only chance for survival was to get him out without delay, and added that, "If we have to carry him he isn't going to make it." We decided that the quickest way, if not necessarily the safest way, was downriver in the canoe. The rest of the ranger rescue team would be hiking upriver from Kyles Landing, so if we met them along the way we could always change over to a carryout. But the idea right now was to get him moving downriver ASAP.

We loaded the patient in my canoe, as the most experienced boater it was up to me to paddle him downriver. The doctor, of course, had the best handle on the medical situation so we made sure he went along in another canoe as we headed downriver. The patient was having difficulty breathing, so we made the decision before starting out that we would closely monitor him as we canoed downriver. If we had any problems we could quickly pull over and allow the doctor to assess and treat the patient.

Ranger George jumped in another canoe and we started off downriver, holding the canoes together in the rapids in a "raft" fashion to give us more stability. We had only gone through a couple of small rapids, about one-fourth miles downriver, when the patient began to convulse. We quickly pulled over to the river right shore onto a flat rock area. The patient was convulsing and gagging, unable to get air into his lungs. Since he was strapped in the litter, and inside on the floor of the canoe we had to pull the litter out and place it on the rock slab to work on him. On shore we turned him on his side to allow any fluids to drain out, and over the next few minutes we did everything possible to help him improve his respirations. Nothing seemed to work, and the gagging and convulsions grew worse. Within about ten minutes of getting him to the river bank the patient stopped breathing but still had a pulse, so we attempted mouth-to-mouth ventilations. The ventilations were still not inflating the patients' lungs. The swelling in the patients' neck had increased dramatically over the past half hour, and, according to the doctor "His neck injury is so severe his trachea must be crushed. We'll never get ventilations into him like this -- I have to do a tracheotomy on him."

This was certainly not a hospital operating room, and we certainly did not have any surgical equipment, so my initial thought (which I kept to myself) was "What, you're going to do a trach here"? But we sprang into action trying to solve the problem of doing a tracheotomy on the river bank. The only "scalpel" we had was my river knife that I kept strapped to my life jacket. I pulled the knife out and handed it to the doctor. I had an oropharyngeal airway in the medical kit, (a curved tube that normally goes in the mouth to assist in ventilating a patient). This airway device would now become a tracheostomy tube, or "trach" tube. The doctor made the incision through the neck and into the trachea and I handed him the airway tube. He inserted it in the neck incision, and then attempted to ventilate; the tube apparently wasn't fitting into the incision property. When he ventilated the air simply would not enter the air passage and inflate the lungs. The doctor attempted ventilations several times with the makeshift trach tube, but it just wasn't working.

At this point the patient had been without respirations for almost two minutes. We didn't have another airway in the medical kit, so I searched around the area for something we could use as a ventilation tube. I found an old plastic milk jug lying in a debris pile on the river bank. The jug had a plastic handle that was about three to four inches long so I cut the handle off and handed it to the doctor. He looked at it and compared the length to the airway tube, the jug handle was about one inch longer than the airway, and was of course a different shape.

The doctor said "well, this isn't sterile procedure, but it may work". He inserted the jug handle into the stoma opening and attempted to ventilate. IT WORKED! Ventilations were getting into the lungs. The doctor continued to ventilate, but the patient did not resume breathing on his own. In fact his pulse had stopped so we had to do both compressions and respirations on him.

We continued to do CPR on the patient for about twenty minutes. After twenty minutes the doctor told us to stop CPR, he checked for a pulse, respirations, or any other signs that the patient was responding. The patient was now cyanotic and there was no indication he was responding to the CPR. The doctor then said "He's gone there's nothing else we can do; I'm going to pronounce him". Noting the time (it was about 7:00pm), the doctor pronounced the patient dead. The doctor went on to say "We did everything we could for him. With his injuries we could have landed on the ER floor when he fell and the outcome would probably have been the same. But we tried. I want to thank you all for your effort".

I thanked the doc for his effort, and still want to thank him every time I think about this incident. This was one of those herculean efforts, way above and beyond the call of duty. Unfortunately the outcome was not the result we hoped for, but the reality is in the emergency service field the outcome does not always have a happy ending.

In fact, throughout my thirty year career as a National Park Ranger I have dealt with hundreds of emergency incidents; the vast majority ended as a "save". But there have also been a number of incidents that have ended in tragedy. The tragedy of dealing with these traumatic incidents does take its toll over time, but you have to keep moving forward, trying to do your best every time.

Just as an emergency worker learns and improves with each incident, you as the public must also learn from these incidents. Please, stay on the trails, obey safety regulations, use good common sense, and unless you have the proper skills and all of the proper safety equipment, never, never, climb on rocks – especially around waterfalls where the rocks are very slick, hard, and very unforgiving.

HEMMED-IN-HOLLOW REVISITED – HISTORY *ALMOST* REPEATS ITSELF

I have been retired from the National Park Service (NPS) since March 31, 2007 but I am still very involved with the Service and I still enjoy a very good relationship with fellow rangers; as they say "once a ranger, always a ranger". I still volunteer at Great Smoky Mountains National Park, still help instruct the NPS High Angle Rescue Classes, and as a certified Swiftwater Rescue Instructor with Rescue 3 International I am still active in instructing swiftwater rescue classes, often for the National Park Service, and particularly at the Great Smoky Mountains NP. Since I still live in Gatlinburg, TN the "Smokies" is in my "backyard". During my thirty year career with the National Park Service I have of course moved around the country from park to park, and I have worked with several rangers who have also moved on to other parks. The NPS is a very small tight knit family and we keep in touch. So I guess its not unusual that on March 21st, 2009 I received a phone call from a District Ranger at Buffalo National River in Arkansas asking me if I could teach a swiftwater rescue class for his park on the Buffalo River, "next week"!

Since I have known the District Ranger for several years I can truly say that he is the epitome of what you would expect a ranger to look like. He's a real character and a real physical specimen with sort of "surfer dude" good looks, so I'll just call him Ranger "Dude". Ranger "Dude" said that the park had put the swiftwater training on the schedule several months ago, a local instructor had been contracted to teach the class but had to cancel at the last minute. Since the class was already scheduled they would like to continue with the training on the pre-set dates if at all possible, hence the question "can you come here and teach it next week? You can stay at my place and the park will pay your expenses to travel". Well, being a retired guy I had to check my busy schedule to see if it would "fit in"; but of course Dude knew the answer before he asked it, of course I'd come and instruct the class. In fact, I was flattered that he would ask. As it turned out there were seventeen participants in the class, most were rangers, a few were resource managers and other park employees, and a couple were Park SAR (Search and Rescue) Team Volunteers.

Rangers practice a foot entrapment rescue technique during a week long swiftwater rescue training course.

I arrived at Dudes' house near Buffalo Point on the Lower Buffalo District the following Sunday and we began to prepare the training that would begin on Monday. This was three days of intense river rescue training; the first day was in the classroom at Park Headquarters, and the second and third days were on the river. To get the best training location that offered some good strong currents and rapids we chose an area in the Upper Buffalo District near the Erbie Campground to do the training. I was staying in the Lower Buffalo District with Dude so we had to rise early and travel for almost two hours to reach the training location, and of course travel "home" for two hours in the evening. The weather was cool both days, with temperatures in the forties and fifties. It rained on the first day we were on the river making it bone chilling. The training was very physically demanding and everyone spent a lot of time in the water doing self-rescue, river crossing, rope, boat handling, and other rescue techniques; in short at the end of the third day of the training we were all physically exhausted. When conducting this type of training we always try to find time during the training to swap a few relevant "war stories" of incidents from the past. This is an excellent way to place emphasis on the techniques being taught by showing examples of what can happen, and allows others to learn and improve from past experiences. Since I had been a ranger at Buffalo National River during the early years of the National River I felt it fitting to share a couple of stories on incidents I had experienced on the Buffalo. One of those "war stories" I told was the previous story about the falling accident at Hemmed-In-Hollow that occurred in 1984 about a young man that had fallen about sixty feet. The story was graphic and illustrated several points on types of incidents that can occur, locating the victim, medical treatment, stabilizing, and backcountry transport and river transport and techniques. That said, as you will learn in a minute, telling that story may have jinxed us.

After we wrapped up the training on the final day, loading all of the gear in the vehicles and putting it back in ready response mode, we held a critique of the training on the riverbank. I was pleased to hear from the group that everyone was very impressed with the quality of the training, good stuff that would come in handy in the future. We wrapped it up at about 4:30 pm, and everyone headed home or to their destination of choice. Several of us had been invited to dinner at one of the volunteer's house, so we stopped off there and had a great meal of white chicken chili – Ozark style, thankful that we didn't have to cook for ourselves again.

Dude and I got to his house on the Lower District about 9:30 pm and after getting cleaned up we put in a movie and sat down to relax. We were both tired from the long and vigorous training over the past three days, but we didn't have to be anywhere early the next day. We decided to wind down and visit for a few minutes since I had to head back home to Tennessee the next day. We were about half way through the movie when the phone rang at 11:30 pm; it was the Park Dispatch Center calling with an emergency message. The report from dispatch was "A MAN HAS FALLEN ABOUT FIFTY TO SEVENTY FIVE FEET FROM A BLUFF AT HEMMED-IN-HOLLOW. WE NEED ALL AVAILABLE PERSONNEL TO RESPOND".

Dude turned to me and said "We have a bad falling accident in Hemmed-In-Hollow, I've got to go, we could use your help – you going with me?" I said, "You bet". So Dude made a couple of coordination phone calls to his ranger staff and to park dispatch for some additional information, and we grabbed our personal packs and gear and headed out the door within a couple of minutes. We made a quick stop by the Buffalo Point Ranger Station and SAR Cache for some additional technical gear, threw it in the truck, topped off the gas tank, and sped out – red lights and siren going.

We were headed to the Compton area, about sixty two miles away over narrow, winding country roads. Luckily at this time of night there wasn't much traffic, but over these roads this was a high speed trip to be remembered. About one hour after leaving Buffalo Point we reached Compton and turned down a narrow gravel road to a trailhead that leads down to Hemmed-In-Hollow. We pulled into the wide trailhead parking lot that had been designated as the Incident Command Post (ICP) and met with the Middle District Ranger who was designated as the Incident Commander (IC). There were also about twelve other rescuers there waiting for the rest of the rescue team members to arrive so we could all be briefed on the mission at one time. We waited a few minutes for a couple of others to arrive, and then the briefing began. What was known at the time was a 22 year old male had been climbing up a cliff wall, he had gotten to a point where he couldn't go up or down so he attempted to jump from the bluff to a nearby tree. He caught a branch on the tree, but the branch broke and he had fallen fifty to seventy-five feet and landed on the rocky forest floor below. He was presently semi-conscious, was in a great deal of pain from his massive injuries, which included a fractured arm, fractured elbow, dislocated hip, broken hip socket, bruised heart, bruised lung, and a possible head fracture. He also had several deep lacerations causing a significant loss of blood. The accident site was several hundred yards off of the main trail and a hasty team led by the Upper District Ranger, several other rangers, a couple of volunteers from a local fire/rescue squad, and two paramedics from AirEvac, a helicopter medical service, were already on the trail trying to locate the victim and his party. The plan called for the hasty team to locate and stabilize the victim. Our team would bring in the litter and additional medical and rescue equipment and begin the transport out by wheeled litter after the hasty team located and stabilized him. The AirEvac helicopter was in an open field beside the ICP. The helo pilot would wait in the area until the patient was brought back to the top and loaded into the helicopter, or we transported him to another suitable Landing Zone (LZ) where the pilot could land and do a pickup of the patient and the flight medics for transport to the hospital.

Our team of fifteen rescuers started down the trail loaded with the wheeled litter, additional medical gear, and technical rope rescue equipment. Hemmed-In-Hollow is located about two and one half miles down the main trail from the Compton Trailhead at the top of the gorge. We then had to take an unofficial side trail for several hundred yards before reaching the waterfalls. The final distance was of course dependent on exactly where the victim was located.

We didn't know exactly where the victim was located when we started down the trail. But about one and one half miles down this steep, slippery and narrow trail we received a radio call from the District Ranger on the hasty team saying that they had located the victim. He was about five hundred to six hundred yards off of the main trail. They had placed flagging tape at a junction in the trail where we would turn left onto a well beaten but unofficial path. From there we would follow the path to where we would meet up with the rest of the victims' party. We continued down the trail to the junction of the flagged path, there we turned left on the path, a really narrow, windy, and slippery trail - this was going to be a tough one. About two hundred yards up the path we met up with the party that had been with the person who fell; they were all huddled around a large fire trying to keep warm. We talked to them briefly and learned that a couple of the folks from their party had gone with the hasty team to lead them to the victims' location. In talking with the leader of the hasty team by radio we found out that the path up to the patient was very steep, rocky, narrow, and generally treacherous. The hasty team leader didn't want to get too many people up on that section of the trail for fear of overcrowding and the possibility of getting any of the rescuers hurt, so we left half of our carryout team at the location with the victims party and half went up to the patient with the litter, ropes and technical rescue gear. By the time we reached the patients location the paramedics with the hasty team had stabilized him on a backboard, splinted and stabilized his arm and leg fractures, stopped and bandaged the bleeding, and had IV's with pain meds and fluids running. With him stabilized on a backboard we began the carry out down the steep slope. The area was very rocky where it ran through a boulder field, with steep drop offs into some drainages. We had to take extra precautions by belaying the patient with ropes and handing off the litter from one group of rescuers to another down a three hundred foot section until we reached the relatively level area where the rest of the team was staged with the patients' party at the campfire. Once we reached the campfire area we transferred the backboarded patient to a Stokes basket litter and fitted a rescue wheel to the bottom of the litter. We took a breather for a few minutes, rotated out the carry out team and headed out toward the main trail.

About twenty minutes later we reached the main trail, it was now about 4:00 am. The two District Rangers that were on scene used the radio to confer with the third District Ranger – who was the IC and on top of the hill. They all agreed that since the patients condition was critical, his only hope of survival was to get him out as quickly as possible. We knew that if we went uphill and back to the trailhead it was going to be two and one half miles of very steep, rugged, terrain. From experience that meant to the rescuer leaders that it would be extremely difficult, and even with about twenty experienced rescuers it would push them to their limit. It also meant that because we would have to use ropes to pull the litter up the trail in several locations we probably couldn't expect to have the patient up to the trailhead before noon.

The second option was to continue downhill toward the river. It was a little longer going downhill, about three miles to the river, but should be a lot faster. Once we reached the river we all agreed that transporting the patient downriver by boat was not an option since all of the available river rangers were on the carryout. There was a designated helicopter landing zone (LZ) on the opposite side of the river, but with the heavy rainfall over the past couple of weeks the river was too high to cross safely with the littered patient. Another option was to take him downhill to a potential LZ at Granny Henderson's which was near the mouth of the river, and on the same side of the river we were on. Granny Henderson's was an old abandoned homesite. It had a large field that potentially could be used as an LZ. If that area was too overgrown with brush and trees we could continue on the trail about one half mile further to Sneed Creek. Sneed Creek had a large flat slab rock area with about two hundred fifty feet of clearing space where a helicopter could land. In considering these two potential LZ's it was decided that the best option was to continue downhill on the trail toward the river, reach one of the LZ sites and have the helicopter meet us there.

We continued down the trail with six on the litter at one time. One group would scout and clear the trail ahead and another would follow behind and fill in on the litter in tight spots as needed, and break each other as needed. Even though we picked the "easiest" route heading downhill, this was no picnic. Several places along the trail were very tight to get the wheeled litter through, and there were several uphill climbs where we traversed down and back up the other sides of drainages. In several places we had to attach a rope to the litter and belay it down over steep pitches. When we got closer to the bottom of the valley we had several creek crossings to make. The water was up quite a bit, the creek bottoms were slick and the water was cold, but everyone jumped in and got their feet wet and we continued on without any problems.

The going was rough, and everyone was exhausted from the physically arduous work as well as the lack of sleep and rest, but we finally made it to the river at about 6:15 am. The river was up really high at the normal crossing. Crossing the river here to get to the normal LZ on the opposite side would have been difficult if not impossible with the littered patient. At the rivers edge we crossed a small stream and paralleled the river for a short distance, then we started back uphill toward Granny Henderson's Field. We reached Granny Henderson's at about 7:00 am, and took a short break while we searched the area for a suitable helicopter LZ. We quickly determined that the area was way too overgrown with small trees, shrubs, and tall grass to allow the helicopter to land there. After a ten minute break we picked up the litter and continued on a rutted path toward Sneed Creek and the second possible LZ.

We knew Sneed Creek was large enough for the helo to land if the creek was within its banks, however, if the creek was badly swollen from the recent rains it might have jumped its banks, reducing the normal size of the LZ on the flat slab rock. The other creeks we had crossed were only moderately higher than normal, so we held out hope that this would be the case with Sneed Creek. About thirty minutes later at 7:40 am we broke out of the forested trail into the open clearing of the Sneed Creek flat rock area. The creek was slightly swollen, and was out of it banks on one side, reducing the LZ by about twenty five percent of its normal size, but the area was a lot wider than I had remembered. It was going to be plenty large enough for the helicopter to land and pick up the patient. The Upper District Ranger used the radio to call for the helicopter to land at the Sneed Creek LZ and within a couple of minutes we could hear the "wop, wop, wop" of the rotors over head. Once the helicopter was within visual site of the LZ, using the radio to talk to the pilot and visual hand signals the helo was marshaled into the LZ by a ranger on the ground team and it landed safely on the flat slab. Once the helo was on the ground the flight medics prepared to bring the patient on board. The patient, still on the backboard, was unloaded from the wheeled litter and secured in the patient compartment of the helo; after assuring that everyone was clear of the aircraft it took off with the patient and the flight medics aboard. After over eleven hours from the time of his accident, including seven hours of a very rough litter carryout, the patient was still holding his own when we loaded him in the aircraft; a testament to the field medical treatment and the skills of the rescue team.

Rescuers load the victim into a medical helicopter after it landed on the slab rock area of Sneed Creek during the rescue of the falling victim at Hemmed-In-Hollow at Buffalo National River. (Photo courtesy of April Wood).

We were all jubilant that we had gotten him safely to the helicopter, and were fairly confident that he was going to survive his injuries once he reached the hospital. The celebration only lasted a few minutes though, because now the reality set in that we had to get ourselves back to civilization. There wasn't going to be a helicopter to come pick us up, no boats to float out on, and no vehicles to pick us up. We had to walk out over four miles up to the top of the gorge with the wheeled litter and all of the medical and technical rescue gear. Everyone was already near exhaustion even before we started the climb out, so we gathered everyone together for a safety briefing reminding everyone to take their time, call for breaks when needed, and help each other along the way. We threw most of the gear inside the litter, strapped it down and started off uphill. It would have been a tough climb out without gear, but with the added weight, lack of sleep, fatigue, lack of food and low on water it was a real test. About three hours later at 11:15 am we were at the trailhead, exhausted, but all safe and uninjured.

At the ICP the IC gathered everyone together for a quick "after action review" of the incident. We learned that the patient had made it safety to the hospital in Little Rock, AR and was scheduled for surgery. He was considered to be in guarded condition but the medical team was optimistic on his outcome.

After a couple of weeks we learned that the patient had done well in the surgeries but it was still too early to tell what his long term recovery would be. We had been tested in this incident and we pulled it off without a hitch, but as always, we also learned what our abilities are and how we can improve. In this type of accident situation we also know that there are lessons that we can pass on to the visiting public to help keep everyone safe. In this case the message is: "Have fun and enjoy the resource but do it in a safe manner. If you are going to climb make sure you have the proper safety equipment, and please never climb on rocks around slippery areas like waterfalls". We also quickly concluded that there were proper ways to descend from a cliff, and that jumping from a cliff to a tree was not a proper technique. In jest we dubbed this technique the "Arkansas Rappel". So in closing, just remember that whatever you do, DON'T EVER ATTEMPT AN ARKANSAS RAPPEL.

LAW ENFORCEMENT IN THE PARKS

Park Service Law Enforcement Shield worn only by Commissioned Law Enforcement Rangers.

"The ranger force is the park police force, and is on duty night and day in the protection of the park. Protection work primarily relates to the care of the forest, the fish and game, the geyser and hot spring formations and the camp grounds. Of equal importance is the detection of violations of the speed laws."
– Horace Albright, Yellowstone Superintendent, 1926.

"I didn't know Rangers carried guns"
–A response by park visitors

WHY DO RANGERS WEAR GUNS?

I wish I had a dollar for every time a shocked park visitor has come up to me and said something like "you guys wear guns, I didn't know park rangers had guns, why do rangers have to carry guns?" Well, let me put the question back to you and ask "would you walk up to a State Trooper, your local County Deputy, or local Policeman and ask the same question?

The simple answer is "park rangers, at least the ones trained to do law enforcement, are the police force of the National Parks". NPS Law Enforcement Rangers are Federal Law Enforcement Officers and are required to complete the Basic Law Enforcement Training for Land Management Agencies at the Federal Law Enforcement Academy in Glynco, GA, a five month course. Immediately after completing the basic training they must complete a three month Field Training Program at a designated park before being assigned to their primary park.

There was a simpler time in the history of NPS, when crime wasn't as rampant and widespread as it is today, when every employee of the NPS had the authority to enforce laws and regulations and make arrest. That doesn't mean that everyone in the NPS did law enforcement work. Even then there were rangers specifically assigned to perform LE duties; even if they didn't have special police training. That all changed in the early 1970's when the NPS realized that those employees conducting law enforcement activities needed special police training, to protect themselves, the public, and to protect the agency from liability.

But that doesn't answer the question of why NPS rangers carry firearms. The simple answer is to protect themselves and the public from harm and criminal activity. But to take it a few steps further just consider that times aren't the same as they used to be, crime is rampant today and criminals don't stop at the park boundaries. Criminals are as likely to be inside the parks as they are outside. They are sometimes actually seeking parks, forest and other outdoor settings for their criminal activity. This may be to prey on unsuspecting tourists, to blend in with the public, or to elude or hide from authorities. Secondly, consider that the National Park Service has the unenviable distinction of having more assaults on Federal Law Enforcement Officers than any other Federal Law Enforcement agency in the nation. Statistics show that a National Park Ranger is three times more likely to be injured or killed on the job than any other Federal employee. Why is that? It has a lot to do with the type of "crime" rangers enforce. Rangers deal with everything from petty offenses to felonies, with the vast majority being minor petty offenses. Therefore, they often don't know that the suspect is even involved in any real criminal activity when they initially approach a person for a minor violation. Most other Federal agencies deal almost exclusively with felonies. When they have to confront a suspect they typically have a warrant, so they know who they are dealing with and are prepared to handle the situation. The funding for the NPS Law Enforcement Program is poor at best, the ranger ranks are grossly understaffed and equipment is in short supply and in need of replacement. It's not uncommon in many parks for one ranger to be on day or night shifts by themselves. If there are other rangers on duty the closest backup from another ranger may be fifteen minutes or more, totally unacceptable for most law enforcement agencies. Also consider the fact that rangers deal in a wide variety of enforcement activities on a routine basis. From vehicle enforcement, hunting/poaching enforcement, backcountry enforcement, disorderly disputes and domestic violence in campgrounds and other areas, burglary, barroom brawls in some park areas, robberies of park visitors and commercial establishments in parks, assaults, and sometimes even murder. Basically every type of law enforcement that a big city police officer, or rural deputy might encounter – but with a lot more possibilities.

As an example, during my first two years as a ranger at New River Gorge NR from 1985 to 1987 I was the only field law enforcement ranger in the park – truly the Lone Ranger. I patrolled the entire park, a length of fifty two miles. The only other law enforcement ranger who could respond as my backup was the Chief Ranger, and he was an administrator, behind a desk at park headquarters. Keep in mind that in the 1980's New River was truly the "wild west". I was constantly running into very volatile people and volatile issues that I had to deal with. I was out there in an old beat up truck that we had gotten as surplus from the Bureau of Reclamation. I had a radio in the vehicle but the park didn't have a law enforcement dispatcher. As a makeshift emergency communications system we had also installed a police scanner in the vehicle. This allowed me to at least listen to the other law enforcement agencies in the surrounding area. If I was lucky I could get hold of a park employee in the visitor center. They could then relay a message by telephone to the county Sheriffs Office if I needed assistance. With the scanner I could at least listen to their response so I would know if backup was responding.

Its unfortunate, but situations like my experience at New River are all too common in the history of the National Park Service.

What's even more unfortunate is the fact that the NPS law enforcement program is still grossly underfunded, and the dangerous situations that rangers face everyday continue to become more frequent. To give you an idea of the variety of threats rangers encounter, below is a collection of some of the types of potentially violent incidents that I, or rangers under my supervision, have dealt with during my thirty year career with the National Park Service:

- **Felon With a Firearm** - New River Gorge National River, July 5, 1998:

A 49 year old Rock Hill, SC man was arrested at Stonecliff Beach for firearms violations, disorderly conduct, alcohol violations, and threatening Federal Officers. A ranger registering campers noticed a black plastic gun case in the bed of the man's pickup. The man was sleeping in his tent at the time so without arousing the man the ranger ran a computer check of the vehicle and the registered owner. The check revealed that the vehicle owner, who was named Johnson, was a fugitive from Oregon and was also a convicted felon. Two additional rangers were called for backup and a felony contact was made on Johnson. During the course of the investigation it was reveled that Johnson was in possession of a .410 gage shotgun and alcohol in a closed area. While under detention by the rangers Johnson became very belligerent, exhibited extreme mood swings, and issued verbal threats to the rangers. It was later determined that he was under treatment for a mental disorder and was not taking his medication. He was arrested and charged with Felon in Possession of a Firearm, Fugitive with a Firearm, Disorderly Conduct, Threatening Federal Officers, and Alcohol Violations.

- **Firearms Violation** - New River Gorge, May 17, 1998:

The Grandview Unit is the home of an Outdoor Drama Theater managed by Theater West Virginia, a professional acting guild that offers several different outdoor dramas throughout the summer months at Grandview. One of the main attractions each year is the play "Hatfield's and McCoy's". The Theater has been practicing the Hatfield's and McCoy's play over the last few weeks. On May 17 the Grandview Unit was packed with visitors at the time and several visitors witnessed a man in a "hillbilly hat and a shotgun" run into the woods near a popular trail shouting "Hatfield's suck". Fearing for their lives the visitors ran to the visitor center and notified rangers. Rangers evacuated the park area, called for backup from the Raleigh County Sheriff Office, and conducted a search of the wooded area for the man. After approximately thirty minutes Rangers observed the man with the gun exiting the woods. He evaded rangers for a few minutes and was then cornered near the outside of the Theater Stage Prop Building and was arrested. In the interview with the suspect it was determined that he was an actor in the Hatfield's and McCoy's production, and after a practice session he suddenly felt the urge to act out the play in real life. It was also determined that the man was currently undergoing treatment for manic-depressant disorders. He had been drinking some during the day, using marijuana, and had not been taking his medication for the mental disorder; this combination apparently triggered the episode. It had also been confirmed that the gun that the suspect had was a stage gun that in the play was loaded to shoot only blanks; however, it could have been easily modified to shoot real ammunition. The actor was charged with Disorderly Conduct.

- **Disorderly Conduct/Firearms Violations** - New River Gorge NR, July 5, 1998:

On July 5, 1998 Rangers contacted a group of Klu Klux Klan members at Helms Beach, a primitive camping area on the upper section of the New River. The purpose of the contact was to conduct a routine camper registration. However during this contact the group admitted that they had several firearms in their possession, two handguns and one shotgun. After explaining the park regulations on the possession of firearms a member of the group who was planning to leave and go back to his residence in North Carolina decided that he would take the guns with him. With the guns removed from the area the rest of the group was allowed to stay in the camp. On the evening of July 6 rangers received a report of a drunk and disorderly group fighting and brandishing firearms from the same camp. A ranger responded along with backup from the WV State Police and re-contacted the group. The group was found to be intoxicated and they were initially belligerent to the Ranger. They also tried some intimidation tactics, like splitting up and attempting to surround the ranger. One of the persons, a man from Landron, NC, who was particularly belligerent, identified himself as member of the security service for the Grand Dragon of the KKK. After securing the group in one location the ranger and trooper found four firearms including two - 9mm pistols, a .45 caliber pistol, and a .308 caliber rifle in a vehicle and their tents. A Stun gun and a "lineman's telephone" with alligator clips was also found and seized. The alleged Klan enforcer and other man were issued citations for possession of firearms. It was determined that the group had just returned from a "Klan" rally in Ohio and on their return trip to NC decided to stop off for a "friendly" camping trip at New River.

- **Disorderly Conduct/Firearms Violations** - New River Gorge NR, July 14, 1998:

On the evening of July 14, 1998 rangers received a report of a disorderly campsite in the Sandstone Falls Campground. According to the reporting party the group was making threatening remarks, drinking heavily, and smoking marijuana. There were only two sites occupied in the campground at the time of the report. One site was occupied by a family group with several children, including one African American female. The other site was occupied by four middle aged white males, two of which were foreign nationals in the U.S. on a visa. When the four men arrived at the campground earlier in the day they had plans for fifteen additional men to arrive the following day. The four men first tried to get the family to move out of their site, saying that it was their site because they camped there every year. When the family refused to move the men became loud and obnoxious but did not press the issue at that time. After setting up their camp the men started drinking heavily, and smoking large quantities of marijuana. The men became very loud and directed derogatory comments, some with racial undertones, back toward the family group. As the night worn on, and as the group became more intoxicated they took a long 1 inch diameter rope, tied a hangman's noose in the end and threw it over the branch of a large tree at their campsite. There were some general comments made by the men about hanging someone, but they were not necessarily directed at the family group. The family, and especially the eight year old African American girl, had become very upset by this time so one member of the family group left the site and drove into Hinton to call for assistance. Rangers arrived on the scene at about midnight and found the four men still up drinking and heavily intoxicated. The rangers conducted a consent search of the campsite, which revealed two concealed handguns, four small baggies of marijuana, and over $1500 in cash divided into four bank bags. Two of the men were charged with Possession of Firearms, and one was charged with Possession of Marijuana; after being cited with the violations the four men were evicted from the campground.

- **Shots Fired at Vehicle** - New River Gorge NR, August 18, 1999

On 8/18 at about 11:46 p.m. West Virginia State Police responded to a report of shots fired in the New Camp area located adjacent to the NPS boundary. Troopers arrived and found that six bail bondsmen, dressed in camouflage clothing, had attempted to stop a vehicle on the Kaymoor road. According to the bondsmen, the vehicle matched the description of a vehicle thought to be driven by a local man who was wanted by the bondsmen for jumping bail on a misdemeanor charge of DUI. The vehicle sped by the bail bondsmen's roadblock and a shot was fired from the vehicle. According to the bondsmen, they returned fire, attempting to shoot out the tires of the fleeing vehicle. After taking statements, the State Troopers released the bail bondsmen and attempted to contact witnesses. While interviewing witnesses from the neighborhood, shots were heard coming from the Kaymoor trailhead parking area within the park boundary. Troopers responded and found that the bail bondsmen had found the vehicle they thought belonged to the bail jumper they were looking for, and had tried to stop it a second time. When the vehicle refused to stop, the bondsmen again shot at the vehicle striking it several times in the trunk and rear window. Because of the proximity to the national park area park rangers were called to assist in the incident and the investigation. Further investigation showed that the suspect vehicle was operated by two brothers of the local man the bondsmen were looking for, but that the man being sought was not in the area. In addition, the second shooting incident had occurred within one hundred fifty feet of a private campground located adjacent to the park boundary. No one was injured in either of the shootings. The investigation continued for two days, and on August 20th the three bail bondsmen were charged with Wanton Endangerment.

• **Discharge of Firearm at Vehicle**- New River Gorge NR, April 4, 1999:

On Saturday 4/24/1999 at about 10:00pm a local man and his girlfriend were driving through the Thayer Bottom area when their vehicle was shot at. The man was driving his white Jeep Cherokee down the Thayer Bottom Road and was approaching the CSX Railroad tracks when a dark colored pickup truck came at high speed from across the tracks and ran them off the road. A man in the other truck yelled at the couple, then jumped out of his vehicle and in a very intimidating manner came toward their vehicle. The couple sped away, but the driver looked back in his mirror just in time to see a flash and hear the gun shot that came from where the man in the pickup truck was standing. The couple continued driving down the dead end road about one hundred yards to a relative's house where he reported the incident to the sheriff's office by telephone. The couples' vehicle was not hit by the gunshot, and no one was injured. The couple was well known in the area, and they didn't think they had any enemies in the area that would be "after them". They were driving a white Jeep Cherokee, and the driver had only been driving the vehicle for about one month. According to him the local residents did not associate the vehicle with the couple. The jeep looks very much like the patrol vehicles driven by NPS rangers in the area, and there was a concern by the NPS rangers that the shooter may have thought he was firing at a Park Ranger.

The shooter was never identified so it was not conclusive that the shooters actual intended target was a ranger. But as the investigation progressed in the days to come evidence uncovered continued to point toward that possibility.

- **Disorderly Conduct/Firearms Violations** - New River Gorge NR, June 6, 1999:

On June 11, 1999 rangers received a report of a disorderly conduct with shots fired on the New River at Terry Beach. Upon arrival at the scene Rangers found about fifteen intoxicated and belligerent local residents on the private in-holding at Terry Beach, a rough establishment known by rangers as 'Jacks' Place'. Rangers learned the fight started when one of the local 'colorful characters', who was intoxicated and was camped on NPS property next to Jacks' Place, thought someone had stolen his cooler full of beer and bologna. 'Colorful' took his axe and went to Jacks Place and demanded his cooler back, allegedly threatening others with the axe. When 'Colorful' refused to leave, Jack (the owner of 'Jacks' Place'), went into his shack and got a shotgun and a semi-auto 9mm handgun. He gave the handgun to his buddy, 'Tough Guy', and kept the shotgun for himself. Jack "asked" Colorful to leave his property several times but Colorful would not comply. Tough Guy then stepped in and threatened Colorful with the handgun, then shot it in the air near Colorful to frighten him. Colorful left and called 911 from his residence, which was close by. After gaining details of the incident, rangers entered Jacks' Place to talk to Tough Guy. There was a large hostile crowd at Jacks' Place when rangers arrived to question Tough Guy. With the support of the belligerent crowd Tough Guy denied any knowledge of the incident and refused to comply with orders given by the Rangers. The situation was becoming threatening so rangers attempted to escort Tough Guy off the property; he resisted and began to fight with the rangers. Pepper spray was used to subdue Tough Guy and he was forcefully removed from the property. Tough Guy was arrested and charged Disorderly Conduct, Interfering with Agency Functions, and Resisting Arrest.

- **Abduction/Armed Robbery** - New River Gorge NR, July 1, 2000:

On July 1, 2000 at approximately 9:30pm, a local man from Oak Hill, WV was fishing on the New River near the Dun Glen Ranger Station when he was abducted and robbed at gunpoint by two black males. The man was driven in his own car to a remote area of the park; his abductors tied him to a tree, left him there, and drove away in his car. After struggling for a couple of hours with the ropes he was able to free himself from his bonds. He walked about five miles to a telephone, and called authorities. The local man's car was recovered on July 3rd in Mount Hope, WV approximately fifteen miles from the scene of the abduction. Much of the valuable property in the vehicle had been taken including a .38 Cal. Revolver that he kept in a cooler.

The local man was able to give rangers and investigators a description of his abductors and composite drawings were made. The case continued for several months, some leads developed but positive identification of the suspects was not conclusive.

- **Discharge of Firearm at Train** - New River Gorge NR, June 24, 2000:

On June 24, 2000 at about 10:30pm rangers responded to a report of a gunshot fired at a train passing through the park along the New River in the Claremont area. The train conductor reported to the CSX dispatcher that while headed west in the area of Claremont someone had fired upon the train. The projectile hit the bulletproof glass on the side of the engine but did not enter the engine compartment. The bullet impacted the glass where the conductor was standing. Ironically the train crew stated that they normally run through this stretch with the windows down, and said that if the window had been down the projectile would have hit the conductor in the chest area. Because of the size of the indentation and the impact made, the conductor thought the projectile was from a large caliber weapon. Rangers investigated and located witnesses who were camping along the New River and had heard the gunshot and a vehicle speed away. The gunshot was most likely fired from the CSX right-of-way, which is easily accessible from McKendree Rd. Witnesses were unable to provide adequate information, and no suspects were identified.

- **Death, Police Shootout** - New River Gorge NR, October 11, 2001:

On October 10th at about 7:20pm a 26 year old South Carolina man was killed in a gun battle with a West Virginia State Trooper while the trooper was conducting a vehicle stop for suspicion of DUI on State Rt. 41 in the community of Prince, within the park boundaries. After making the stop the trooper brought the suspect back to his cruiser and placed him in the back seat, without searching or restraining him. The trooper radioed dispatch for an NCIC check on the South Carolina registration, and was in the process of filling out a written warning for weaving on the roadway when the dispatcher came back over the radio with a "hit" for a stolen vehicle out of South Carolina. Hearing the dispatchers report the man bolted out of the back door of the vehicle. As he was exiting the cruiser he drew a .38 caliber revolver from a shoulder holster and from just outside of the cruiser fired at least one round at the trooper (two rounds were expended from this revolver), hitting the rear window and the door post. The man then ran up to his vehicle and demanded his other gun from his girl friend, a 14 year old girl (who it was later determined to be a runaway). She handed him a .45 caliber semi-auto handgun. The man then turned toward the cruiser and started firing rounds at the driver's seat and the trooper. Three rounds hit the cruisers windshield and hit in the area of the driver's seat of the troopers' vehicle. At least four other rounds hit the hood area of the cruiser. By this time however, the trooper had bailed out of his patrol car and ran around to the right rear of the vehicle using the vehicle for cover. A gun battle developed in the roadway with both parties exchanging gunfire. The man then ran to his vehicle, a Jeep Cherokee, and sped away. The trooper continued to fire at the fleeing Jeep, hitting and shattering the rear window.

Ranger Harry was on patrol in the vicinity at the time, actually driving on a road just across the river, and saw the cruisers blue lights and then heard the gunshots. He arrived on scene within one minute of the shots being fired. When ranger Harry pulled up to the cruiser he got a quick briefing from the trooper on what had happened. They noticed that the Jeep had stopped along the roadway about two hundred yards up the road from the shooting site. After calling for assistance ranger Harry and the trooper proceeded on foot up the road toward the Jeep. They thought that the man had left his vehicle and ran into the surrounding woods so they approached the vehicle with caution. About twenty minutes after the shooting they reached the Jeep and found the man was still in the drivers' seat, but he was dead.

During the shootout the trooper had fired at least six rounds into the rear of the vehicle, five of those rounds had entered into the back of the victims' seat, with at least three hitting him. The 14 year old female was uninjured in the gunfire. When the Jeep came to a stop she had jumped out and ran down the road to a house to get help; the residents brought her back to the scene.

- **Felon With Firearms, Stolen Vehicle, Stolen Firearms** - Great Smoky Mountains National Park, May 19, 2002:

While in route to provide backup to another ranger who was on a DUI stop on the Foothills Parkway Spur, a ranger came upon a van on the Gatlinburg Bypass with a muffler dragging and shooting sparks along the roadway. After calling in the vehicle registration to park dispatch, the ranger made a vehicle stop on the van. The ranger quickly explained the hazard to the female driver, and the male passenger jumped out of the vehicle and hastily repaired the muffler with a piece of wire. The ranger cleared the stop and continued his response to other rangers' location on the Foothills Parkway Spur to assist in the DUI stop. Almost immediately after clearing the stop the ranger received a "hit" on the van from dispatch, the hit showed that the van had been stolen from Garden City, SC. The ranger turned around, quickly relocated the van, and followed it northbound on the Foothills Parkway Spur. He had intended to stop the van in the vicinity of where the other ranger on the DUI stop was so he would have immediate backup, however the driver of the van refused to stop.

The ranger was finally able to get the van pulled over just before reaching Pigeon Forge and the end of the Parkway Spur. The ranger approached the van from the passenger side, surprising both the passenger and the driver. He then brought the passenger out of the vehicle handcuffed him and put him in his vehicle without any problems. A Pigeon Forge Police officer arrived as backup and assisted in handcuffing and arresting the female driver.

Criminal history checks from dispatch confirmed that the vehicle was stolen, and showed that both the man and the woman were fugitives from justice from North Carolina on the charge of "Burglary/forced entry while using a handgun". It was further discovered that the male passenger was a convicted felon and had served a prison sentence for a violent crime involving a firearm. A search of the van revealed a .40-calibre semi-auto pistol with two loaded magazines under the passenger seat, and a TEC-DC9 9-mm machine gun type pistol, with a silencer and two loaded magazines on the seat behind the drivers compartment. It was further discovered that the TEC-9 pistol was a stolen firearm.

Both suspects were arraigned in Federal Court on charges of Fugitive in Possession of a Firearm. The driver was charged with Possession of a Stolen Vehicle, and the passenger was charged with Felon in Possession of a Firearm. Both were also charged with violations concerning the stolen firearm and illegal firearms charges were pursued through assistance from ATF.

Illegal firearms, (40 caliber semi-auto pistol and a 9mm "tec-9" machine gun type pistol) seized from two convicted felons in Great Smoky Mountains NP in May 2002.

As the District Ranger I reviewed the incident, and as part of the review I looked at the in-car video in the rangers patrol vehicle. The video clearly showed that when the ranger initially stopped the van on the Gatlinburg Bypass for the muffler problem the ranger was kneeling down behind the van talking to the van's passenger, who was in the process of wiring up the muffler. The driver came out of the van and with her right hand behind her back she crept back to the rear of the van to where she could see the ranger. It appeared that she was about to pull something from her waistband but suddenly stopped. She turned around and crept back toward the front and got back in the drivers seat. Luckily, just as she peered around the corner of the van the passenger finished with the makeshift repair, the ranger stood up, talked for a moment with the passenger, and then got back in his patrol car to leave. The body language of the female driver on the video clearly showed that her intentions were to attack the ranger with a firearm or other weapon, but stopped when the ranger suddenly decided to clear the scene. During the interview with the driver she denied that she had any intentions of attacking the ranger.

- **Ginseng Poaching, Firearms Violation** - Great Smoky Mountains NP, September 2003:

While driving on Newfound Gap Road in the Sugarlands area, and near park headquarters ranger Heath noticed a man and his 16 year old son come out of the woods and began walking up the road. According to ranger Heath the two just didn't look like typical hikers. Heath was suspicious so he turned his vehicle around and drove back to talk to them. As he approached, the two quickly crossed the road and hurried down an embankment toward the Little River. Heath got out of the patrol car and went down the embankment behind them; he found them at the river standing near a large boulder. The man and boy were identified as father and son, they appeared evasive, and when questioned they refused to discuss what they were doing in the area. However the man did say that they had not been doing anything illegal and that they did not have any drugs or firearms with them. Ranger Heath looked around the immediate area and found a muddy backpack hidden behind the large boulder, he asked the pair if it was theirs and they said that it was "not theirs". Heath checked and inside the backpack he found 50 freshly dug ginseng roots.

Ranger Michael arrived to assist and when he questioned the father he eventually admitted ownership of the backpack and the fifty ginseng roots. He also admitted that they had dug up and collected several other ginseng roots and hid them along the trail when they ran down the embankment to evade the ranger Heath. The father took ranger Michael back up the trail and showed him where he had dumped the roots; ranger Michael collected an additional one hundred and five roots from the pile. The father also admitted that he had been carrying a handgun with him. He took ranger Michael back to the large boulder and on the opposite side of the rock from where the backpack had been. There the rangers found a loaded two-shot .38 caliber derringer hidden in a crevice of the boulder. The father was charged with Preservation of Natural Features and Possession of a Firearm. The ginseng roots were turned over the park's Science and Natural Resource Division and were replanted in the park's forest environment.

Rangers often have to deal with a variety of resource crimes involving natural and cultural resources. The photo above shows weapons and equipment that were collected in one case of ginseng poaching (top left), the ginseng roots that were stolen (upper right), a pickup truck load of moss poached from the Great Smokies Mountains NP (lower left), and a deer poached and only a small portion harvested by the poachers (lower right).

- **Ginseng Poaching / Possession of Firearm,** Great Smoky Mountains National Park, September 27, 2003:

On September 27, while on patrol on Rt. 32 on the east side of the park, ranger Paul noticed a car parked near the Gilliland Cemetery. This area contains a large amount of American Ginseng, and has a past history of extensive Ginseng poaching. Based on these facts ranger Paul decided to set up surveillance on the vehicle and called for another ranger to assist him. Ranger Paul and his backup ranger Steve concealed themselves in the wooded area and waited for the owner to return. After a short wait the owner of the vehicle, a 32 year old man from Sherills Ford, NC walked out of the wooded area of the park and returned to the vehicle. As the man approached the vehicle the rangers noticed he was carrying what appeared to be a digging stick in one hand and plant material in the other. The rangers ordered the man to stop and get down on the ground; he complied with the order without resistance. They found that the plant material he was carrying in his hand was American Ginseng tops, seventy nine freshly dug Ginseng roots were found in the mans front cargo pants pocket and one hundred and six ginseng berries were found in his shirt pocket. They also found that the man had in his possession a marijuana pipe and a small quantity of marijuana. The man was not armed at the time he was stopped coming out of the park, but a consent search of his vehicle revealed a loaded .22 caliber rifle in his vehicle. The man also admitted that he had camped at the Cosby Campground the previous night but had not paid for the campsite. The man admitted that he had come to the National Park specifically for the purpose of digging Ginseng. He was charged with "Gathering and Possessing Ginseng", "Possession of Controlled Substance" and "Driving on a Suspended License".

- **Ginseng Poaching / Possession of Firearm, Great Smoky Mountains National Park, October 4, 2003:**

On October 4th, while on patrol in the Big Creek area, ranger Steve noticed a vehicle backed in a wooded area at Browns' Cemetery, just outside of the park boundary. Because the vehicle was parked in a location of previous ginseng poaching activity ranger Steve decided to set up surveillance on the vehicle. He hid his vehicle, got his camouflage clothing from his vehicle and walked into the woods inside the park boundary. Steve was getting ready to put on the camo clothing when he heard someone walking toward him through the woods from inside the park. He quickly hid behind a large tree and watched two men in full camouflage clothing walk within twenty five feet of him, they then dropped to their knees apparently preparing to dig in the ground with a tool. Ranger Steve then came from behind the tree, identified himself, and ordered the two men to stop and get on the ground. Both men immediately jumped up and starting running in opposite directions. Ranger Steve followed one man, a 46 year old man from Boone, NC. The man ran through the woods about fifty yards and came out of the park onto State Rt. 32. He ran into a large culvert under the road, and came out of the culvert on the downhill side of the road. Steve chased the man through the woods, went on top of the road and cut him off after he came out of the culvert, catching up to and apprehending him about one hundred yards on the downhill side of the road.

After handcuffing the man, Steve searched him and found a loaded .22 caliber handgun in the top pocket of his bib overalls. No Ginseng was found on him at the time of his apprehension, and when asked if he had or had taken any Ginseng from the park he said "no". Three other rangers arrived to assist ranger Steve, and using mantracking techniques they back-tracked his movements and located a plastic baggie near Rt. 32 that contained eighty three American Ginseng roots. The roots were freshly dug and still had moist dirt on them. The man was arrested and charged with "Gathering and Possessing Ginseng Plants", "Interfering with Agency Functions", and "Possession of a Concealed Weapon" and was placed on a $5000 bond. The man's companion was able to elude the rangers, and was not apprehended.

- **Possession of Marijuana with Intent to Distribute,** Great Smoky Mountains National Park, July 19, 2003:

On the afternoon of July 19, ranger Greg contacted a 25 year old Knoxville, TN man on the bank of the East Prong of the Little Pigeon River in the Greenbrier area of the Park. The man had been swimming in the river with some friends just prior to the contact. The area is closed to the possession and consumption of alcoholic beverages, and as ranger Greg approached the man he noticed he was drinking beer. Greg was in the process of writing the man a citation for possession of alcoholic beverages when he noticed that he was acting suspiciously and seemed to be paying particular attention to his backpack, which was lying nearby. Greg was concerned that the backpack may contain weapons so he picked up the backpack and walked the man out toward the patrol vehicle. While carrying the backpack from the river bank to his patrol vehicle Greg noticed that there was a very strong odor of marijuana coming from the backpack, so when he reached the vehicle he conducted a search of the backpack. Inside the backpack he found a large plastic baggie containing several smaller baggies of prepackaged marijuana. The backpack contained a total weight of 4.74 ounces of marijuana. The man later admitted that he sold marijuana and that some of the packages sold for $90, and some sold for $100. He was charged with Possession of Marijuana, Possession of Marijuana with Intent to Distribute, and Possession of Alcohol Beverages in a Closed Area.

- **Assault On A Federal Officer,** Great Smoky Mountains National Park, February 27, 2003

During the early morning hours of February 27, 2003, two rangers and two maintenance employees, were working traffic control and tree removal on the Foothills Parkway Spur after a winter storm had caused numerous trees to fall down across the roadway. At 1:00am one of the rangers who was directing traffic observed a vehicle traveling northbound towards him at a high rate of speed, the vehicle was traveling directly at him and was not going to slow down. The ranger had to jump onto the road shoulder to avoid being struck by the vehicle. As the vehicle flew pass him he was able to read a partial tag and vehicle type and relay the information and a warning to the second ranger who was stationed with two maintenance workers about three hundred yards further down the road and around a bend. The second ranger and the maintenance workers also had to jump out of the way, and also barely avoided being hit by the vehicle as it sped by and continued on down the road. The second ranger quickly ran to her vehicle and was able to locate the vehicle and get the vehicle stopped in the nearby city Pigeon Forge.

The investigation revealed that the driver was under the influence of alcohol (BAC 1.9%), and driving on a suspended license. He was arrested, posted bail two days later and returned to his residence in Cleveland, OH. When his court appearance came up about three months later he failed to appear in Knoxville for the proceedings. A warrant was issued and he was arrested in Cleveland, OH and brought back to Knoxville for trial. He was found guilty of DUI, and Assault on a Federal Officer.

- **Armed Robbery, Great Smoky Mountains National Park -**
August 26, 2006

On the evening August 26, 2006 two Maryville College students were sitting in their car at an overlook on the Foothills Parkway when two armed men assaulted and robbed them. Albert Reynolds and Michael Babineau, both local men from Maryville, TN drove up to the overlook at a high rate of speed, stopped abruptly, jumped out of their car and ran up to the students car. Reynolds was wielding a large tire iron; he threatened the couple, ordered them out of their car, and demanded money from them.

The couple did not have any money on them, so they handed over their wallets and a cell phone to the assailants hoping that they would be satisfied and leave. That didn't satisfy them, and after handing over their personal property Reynolds then demanded the female victim to remove her clothing. She refused to undress so Reynolds and Babineau pushed the man and woman to the ground, threatened and intimidated them, then quickly jumped in their car and fled the scene. Luckily, as they pulled away the victims were able to get the license number of their assailant's vehicle.

Reynolds and Babineau didn't get any cash from the victims but they did get credit cards. Once they realized they had the cards they drove almost directly to the local Wal-Mart in Maryville, TN and charged over four hundred dollars on the victim's credit card. Since they no longer had a cell phone, the couple drove to the Maryville Police Dept. to report the incident.

Since the incident occurred in the Great Smoky Mountains National Park, Maryville Police Department called park dispatch to report the crime. A ranger and an NPS Special Agent immediately began an investigation. Along with the lead on the vehicle, video footage was obtained showing the subjects at Wal-Mart purchasing items with the stolen credit card. Babineau, who was driving his father's vehicle at the time of the assault, was tentatively identified through the video footage.

On September 1, after extensive investigation, arrest warrants were issued for Babineau and Reynolds as well as search warrants for their residences. Babineau was taken into custody and during a subsequent interview he confessed to his role in the incident. Reynolds had fled the area and was arrested on September 23rd by Knox County Sheriff Department on the arrest warrant and other unrelated charges. Reynolds was interviewed by the ranger and special agent and confessed to his role in the incident.

Both subjects pled guilty to armed robbery and assault charges in US District Court. At the March, 2007 sentencing hearing, Albert Reynolds, who was classified as a career criminal by federal standards, received one hundred and twenty five months incarceration, followed by three years of supervised release. Babineau received twenty four months incarceration, followed by three years of supervised release.

Marijuana Eradication, New River Gorge NR, August 10 - 12, 1992:

On August 10, 11, and 12 rangers participated in a major marijuana eradication effort on the New River Gorge NR, Gauley River NRA and surrounding counties (Raleigh, Fayette and Nicholas). This was a joint effort coordinated by the National Park Service, Fayette Co. Sheriff Dept., and WV State Police. A helicopter from the Wood Co. Sheriff, operating under a federal grant, was used to locate marijuana plantations throughout the area. Over the three day period nine different plantation sites containing a total of ninety six plants were found inside and outside of the boundaries of New River Gorge NR and Gauley River NRA, using a helicopter as the primary means to locate the plantations.

A ground crew made up of rangers, deputies and troopers then moved in and eradicated the plants. This was a pure eradication effort, and it was not expected that any growers would be arrested, and as expected no arrests were made, but some leads developed for future efforts.

During the operations two noteworthy incidents occurred during the eradication effort:

- On 8/11 while flying over an area that was suspected to be a grow site, the helicopter observer thought he saw a small patch of marijuana plants along the powerline. The helicopter made a wide turn back toward the area when they noticed a man run from a nearby residence and into the woods toward where they thought they spotted the marijuana. At about the same time a second man ran out of the house and jumped on a tractor with a brush hog attached and raced across a field. The observer and pilot lost site of the tractor when it entered a wooded area. They next saw the tractor along the edge of the wood line and powerline where the man was running the brush hog, and traveling very fast along a section approximately fifty yards long. The tractor then returned to the area where it was originally parked outside of what appeared to be the curtilage of the residence, the driver left the tractor and ran into the house. The pilot flew the helicopter back over the area but after the tractor mowed the area they were unable to find any marijuana plants in the area where they had previously thought they had seen the plants.

A marijuana garden of about 150 plants as viewed from a helicopter during a marijuana eradication detail. The marijuana is the patch of darker vegetation in the upper center of the photo surrounded by bare soil. (Courtesy of the National Park Service)

- On 8/12 a ranger was serving as aerial observer, on a highly suspect farm on the boundary of the Gauley River NRA, when she and the pilot observed a man lay what appeared to be a pistol on the hood of his truck and aim it at the helicopter. The pilot reported the incident to the ground crew and immediately left the area. The owner of the farm is known to have grown marijuana in the past, had a history of violent behavior and had made verbal threats to police officers in the past.

Marijuana eradication, even though it rarely nets the arrest of growers, is a very successful method of eliminating and discouraging illegal drug activity. As shown in this story, it can also help to develop information on suspects, and it can be dangerous.

Murder - Great Smoky Mountains NP, January 13, 2006:

On January 15, 2006, hikers found the body of a young female in the woods approximately twenty yards off of the Toms Branch Road, which is located in the Deep Creek area of the Great Smoky Mountains National Park. Rangers, an NPS Special Agent, and Swain County deputies responded to the scene and initiated an investigation. Due to darkness, the scene was protected until the next morning when the FBI joined the investigation. The preliminary investigation found that she had been shot twice in the face and that the murder had occurred at the same location as where the body had been found. Initially the identity of the female was unknown since there were no missing person reports matching the description of the victim. The Cherokee Tribal Police Department joined into the intensive investigation; this led to identification of the body as a 17 year old female who was an enrolled Cherokee tribal member of the Cherokee Nation.

The investigation led to the January 20th arrest of Terrence Roach, age 20, who was also a tribal member. Roach confessed to the murder and stated that he and another person had driven the victim into the park on January 13th and shot her with a .38 caliber revolver. On January 24, two other tribal members Michael Slee, age 19 and Joshua Squirrel, age 18 were arrested and charged with "Accessory after the fact to Murder". A U.S. Magistrate Judge ordered all three men to be held without bond, Roach was later convicted in Federal Court of Murder, Slee and Squirrel were convicted to Accessory after the fact to Murder. According to Roach and the other involved persons the murder followed a drug party. Roach had suspected the 17 year old female of stealing some of his drugs during the party. As "pay back" he took her for a drive in the park and after a brief argument he executed her.

RELIC HUNTING – VIOLATOR
HAS THE "BLUES"

I worked as a seasonal Forestry Technician with the U.S. Forest Service on the George Washington National Forest for three seasons, from 1974 through the spring of 1978. Over those three seasons I worked in almost every forest management field the U.S. Forest Service had to offer. From forestry, recreation management, backcountry management, fire management, and land surveying. I loved the variety the job offered, and was sure I had found the career of my dreams. However, a seasonal position doesn't guarantee you will have a job from season to season and there are no benefits with seasonal positions like there are with permanent positions. Basically, as far as the job went it was my dream job, but the reality was it had no real job security. Linda, my wife, was a nursing student at the time and working part time as a Nurses Aid. She had no benefits either, and we had a young family that depended on us. It took a severe case of appendicitis, one that put me in the hospital for ten days, for me to realize that I needed to get a permanent position. Since we had no medical insurance, this little problem left us with about two thousand dollars in medical bills.

I started applying for permanent positions on the Federal level as a Forestry Technician and Park Technician, which would most likely be in the USFS or the National Park Service. I fully expected, and hoped that with a degree in Natural Resource Management, and three seasons of experience with the USFS that I would be more qualified for Forestry Technician jobs with the US Forest Service than I was for Park Technician positions with the USNPS. However, when my Civil Service rating scores came back I qualified out with a score of 100 as a Park Tech, and in the low 80's for Forestry Tech positions with the USFS – go figure, sounds like the government doesn't it? Well anyway during the spring of 1978, while I was still recovering from my bout with appendicitis, I received three different job offers from the National Park Service, all three with "National Military Parks". I would have jumped all over an offer from Shenandoah NP, which was close to where we lived at the time. I was very familiar with Shenandoah NP, but a "Military Park" was a different animal and I didn't quite know what to make of it. I had put my time in with the military, actually getting a three month early out in 1973 after the U.S. pulled out of Vietnam; I had no interest in going back to the military.

When I received the third offer it was for the Fredericksburg and Spotsylvania National Military Park in Fredericksburg, VA. I hadn't been to Fredericksburg but thought it was near Quantico, so I naturally associated it with the Marine Corps Base. I had been in my current seasonal position with the USFS from June to April of that year, milking it through the winter and extending it for almost a year. The position was running out in one month and I had to make a decision, and soon. I decided to give Fredericksburg a look. I had already been offered the position sight un-seen and without an interview. Before making a decision on whether or not to accept the job I decided that I was going to "interview" the park. I arranged a meeting with an official at the park and we drove down the following week to meet with him. When I walked into his office in Chatham Manor I was met by the Chief Park Ranger. I was amazed to find out that he was actually a uniformed ranger in the National Park Service. We had a short visit in the office where he explained that the job was a law enforcement ranger position in the Resource and Visitor Protection Division. He explained that if I took the position I would basically be a protector of the treasures of the national battlefields as well as the park visitors. We also took a tour around the park to the four battlefields – Fredericksburg, Chancellorsville, Spotsylvania, and Wilderness - and stopped by for a look at the ranger residence my family and I would be living in if I accepted the position. Linda and I had a quick discussion and then I accepted the position. I had a permanent position in the National Park Service, and even though reluctantly at first, one that I grew to love.

Attending and completing the law enforcement academy was required for the position, but there was a backlog of new rangers awaiting training in the Federal Law Enforcement Training Academy – FLETC. It was almost one year later before I got my bid to attend. The time between entering the position and attending FLETC gave me an opportunity to learn the mission of the NPS, and to learn the park very well. I became the "jack of all trades" for the ranger division, doing resource management work, interpretation, and safety inspections and a variety of other odd jobs that are handed to the ranger division. One of these "odd jobs" came during the summer months when I was selected to work as the project supervisor with the Youth Conservation Corps, a residential youth program the park managed. I also spent a good deal of time in the "backcountry" areas of the park. During these backcountry trips I began to find evidence that there was relic hunting activity in every battlefield in the park. I quickly realized that we had a problem that needed to be addressed.

After completing Basic Law Enforcement Training at FLETC in September of 1979 I returned to the park ready to go to work addressing law enforcement issues. From the perspective of Park Management most of the problems and complaints that they addressed came from traffic accidents and traffic control issues. So, most of the rangers in the park spent their time on road patrol, behind the wheel of a patrol car and with a good portion of it running radar. I did my share of road patrol, but it didn't take me long to realize that I didn't want to be a full time highway patrolman. I also saw the need to do resource protection work, and the truth is that's where my real interests were.

Shortly after returning from the academy hunting season got into full swing. At the time there was a large whitetail deer population in the area and even though hunting is prohibited within the park there was heavy hunting pressure all around the edges of the park. Poaching was a fairly frequent occurrence from some of the back roads in the park. It was also legal to run deer with dogs in the surrounding counties. Often dogs were turned loose in or near the park by less than honest hunters and allowed to run through the park. These hunters would then wait along the boundary for the deer to run out of the park and "take" them as they exited the park; sometimes shooting into the park or across park roads. This was not only hard on the deer and other wildlife populations in the park but it was also hazardous to park visitors. I worked several good hunting and poaching cases that season, most of them in the Wilderness and Chancellorsville Battlefields.

One case in particular involved four hunters that entered the park on the backside of a farm on the Wilderness Battlefield. A local landowner had called in the report of the illegal hunters on park property. I got the call and I was there waiting for them as they walked deeper into the park. During this same season, I was also shot at while driving along a road in a patrol car; now it was getting personal.

The time I had spent getting familiar with the park and the wildlife cases I had worked during my first year out of the academy was beginning to pay off, and it set the stage for future resource protection work. Our park battlefields, where brothers fought brothers, are the most hollowed grounds in the U.S. and are strictly protected by laws and regulations. The use of relic detectors, digging, and theft of artifacts on these park areas is strictly prohibited.

Even with the prohibition and the strict enforcement, there are those that will still take advantage of these sacred resources for their own personal greed. It only took a couple of months of exploring the backcountry areas before I began to find evidence of recent relic hunting. The first evidence I found was in the Wilderness Battlefield - small freshly dug holes. I noticed that the holes in this area were mostly dug on and near the earthworks; a real shame since these are irreplaceable resources. Nature already takes a severe toll on the historic earthworks in the park; digging in them dramatically accelerates natural erosion process. After finding the digging I came back to the area once a week. I tried to alternate my days of the week in an effort to find the culprits doing the digging. Hopefully this would allow me to at least put a pattern to when they were digging and where they were entering the park. This area was being worked periodically, about once every one to two months which made it hard to establish a pattern. After having no luck in the Wilderness I moved on to Spotsylvania and Chancellorsville Battlefields to do a quick check for activity there. I could only allot about one day a week to the resource protection work so it took a while to get around the battlefields and find any activity. But after about three weeks of looking I finally found some fairly recent digging in the Chancellorsville Battlefield. This area was only about one half mile from my residence so I could check on it almost every day. Over a period of about five weeks I found freshly dug holes on the Chancellorsville site on three different occasions. A pattern was beginning to form; it appeared that the digging activity in this area was likely happening on Thursdays or Fridays.

On Friday of week six I drove by the area and noticed an unfamiliar vehicle parked along the state road near the area where I had found the relic hunting activity. I decided to check it out and entered the area along the boundary, walking very slowly and watching for any movement. After only about ten minutes I began to hear occasional sounds of what might be a shovel digging in the ground, and then I heard voices. I was stationary, but the sounds seemed to be getting closer so I stepped behind trees and brush and watched and waited. Suspecting that these may be the culprits I had been looking for I used my handheld radio to call for backup. Bill, my supervisor was about twenty minutes away and said that he was headed my way. Within another ten minutes I saw the movement of two people; they were about thirty yards apart and moving slowly in my direction. I watched as they both used a metal detector to sweep the ground and saw both of them use a small shovel and dig in the ground. On two occasions I saw them reach into the hole, remove something and place the items in a pouch or pocket. As they got closer I noticed that both of them were wearing camouflage clothing, and the metal detectors they were using were also camouflaged. It was apparent that they were not amateurs. They were going to extremes to conceal themselves, being very stealthy and communicating mostly by hand signals or in a near whisper.

I continued to watch them from cover as they moved in my direction. I didn't know who I was dealing with or how they would react at getting arrested. So my plan was to wait until my backup arrived before revealing myself. However, at this point I was in a bit of a pickle, if I moved they were going to see me and run – or worse. If I didn't make a move they were going to walk right into me. As they continued forward it also became more apparent that they were probably headed back to their vehicle. I decided it was time to make my move. While standing behind a large tree that I was using for cover I called for both of them to stop. I identified myself as a U.S. Park Ranger and ordered them to place their items they had in their hand on the ground, to turn away from me and kneel on the ground. The man in the lead looked at the second person and it looked to me like he was getting ready to run. I shouted for him to stop and advanced on him. He then stopped and knelt down as ordered, the second man also complied.

I radioed my situation to my supervisor and found that he was just arriving along the road and was about one hundred yards away from my location. These two men were adults and at least the younger one was projecting a threatening posture. The younger one was about forty years old and appeared to be the leader, the older man was in his fifties and was being cooperative. As soon as I approached them the younger man said "you're making a mistake, you don't want to do this". I told him he was engaged in an illegal activity and that "I do want to do it". After a quick search of both of the men and finding no weapons, except for the military type hoe/shovel one of them had, I walked them out of the woods to the vehicles. Ranger Bill met us half way. As we were walking out, and before we were met by ranger Bill the younger man again said "you're making a mistake, you don't know who I am – you'll regret this".

I just ignored this last comment and continued to walk them out, but I thought "we'll find out soon enough who you are".

Neither of the two men had identification on them, saying that they had it in their vehicle. Sure enough the suspicious vehicle I had seen parked along the road when I entered the woods was theirs, so when we returned to the vehicle I had them get their ID out. That's when I found out what he meant by the "you're making a mistake... you'll regret this" comment. The younger of the two men retrieved his wallet from his vehicle and immediately flashed his badge on me. The badge and credentials identified him as a Federal Law Enforcement Officer from another agency and was stationed in Washington, DC – a brother in blue. I was shocked at being "badged", especially by the fact that he was a Federal Law Enforcement Officer, but I tried not to let it show. Now don't get me wrong here, I understand the unwritten code on professional courtesy, but that normally extends to traffic violations. This was much different, and in many respects no different than if a law enforcement officer broke into a home or vehicle and stole items from it. In my opinion the theft of our national heritage is about as bad as it gets. It's bad enough when a typical criminal is involved but the fact that a trusted Federal Law Enforcement Officer – of an agency very close to mine – would stoop so low and be so calculating cut deeper. This was downright dishonest and disloyal to us all, his agency, his fellow officers, and the citizens of the U.S. I was not going to let this go without a fight and I told my supervisor that right then and there. He agreed and said he would stand behind me. As it turned out the other man with the officer was his neighbor, he just stood by and watched the whole exchange without comment; I'm sure he was hoping for a break.

Today with the enactment of the Archeological Resource Protection Act (ARPA) both of these men could have been charged with a felony, with a potential punishment of a $20,000 fine or two years imprisonment or both. At the time though all we had to charge them with was a violation of the Code of Federal Regulations (CFR) a petty offence with a potential punishment of $5,000 fine or six months or both. I wrote both of the men up for CFR violations for Destruction of Park Resources (the digging), Use of a Metal Detector, and Theft of Govt. Property (the Minie balls I found in their possession). This was a cite and release situation so after writing both of them mandatory appearance citations, confiscating their metal detectors and equipment, and confiscating the stolen items they were allowed to go on their way, but with a promise to appear in Federal Court in two months.

Two months later I appeared in court on the case. My supervisor and I had to meet with the Assistant U.S. Attorney (AUSA) prior to the case to brief him on the details. As it turned out there was to be no briefing. The AUSA already knew the details of the case, knew that one of the persons involved was a Federal Law Enforcement Officer. Then he dropped the bomb. The AUSA refused to try the case. He said that he was going to dismiss the case on both persons. My supervisor and I both argued that it was a gross violation of Federal Law, especially for a sworn Federal Law Enforcement Officer, and that it would be an injustice to let him and his partner get by without a trial. But he still refused to send the case before the judge. When we asked him why he felt it should be dismissed he said simply "because his agency brings more and better cases to this court" than the National Park Service does, and he "is not going to loose the support of the agency by embarrassing them". When we asked him why he was dismissing the case on the other person, he said that he "couldn't dismiss one case and not the other", simple as that. The AUSA said that the officers' agency was going to take internal action on him, that he would be dealt with by his own. But, the other guy was getting off scot free.

The AUSA has the discretion to dismiss any case he sees fit. Normally that only happens if it's a bad case, one laden with mistakes on the charging officers' part, lack of evidence, or poor case preparation. None of these were the case on this one. We told the AUSA that we disagreed and would like to follow up with the Federal Magistrate that was scheduled to hear the case. He didn't like it but conceded that it was our right to do so. Immediately after our meeting with the AUSA Bill and I marched down the hall and met with the Federal Magistrate. He was contrite on hearing the details but said it was up to the AUSA to bring the case forward. He said it was the prerogative of the US Attorneys Office to dismiss cases and he couldn't do anything unless the case came before him. The AUSA had made up his mind to dismiss the case and try as we may there was nothing we could to prevent it, so we had to walk away.

I had learned several very valuable lessons from this incident concerning politics and how the "system" worked, and that not all persons sworn to uphold the law can be trusted. I also learned that when someone says "you're making a mistake" or "you'll be sorry", that's a clue; get ready for the other shoe to drop. These were hard lessons but ones that I would remember for the remainder of my career.

As I walked away from the court that day, even though I was disappointed in the outcome, I was resolved to make the best of these lessons. I became determined to clean up the theft of our parks natural and cultural resources. If this case did anything it made me a martyr for the cause. During the remainder of my time at Fredericksburg and Spotsylvania NMP, while still working my share of typical "front country" law enforcement I continued to put a major emphasis on the backcountry issues. I worked several other several significant wildlife poaching cases and six very significant relic hunting cases that occurred in all four of the battlefields in the park. This time the cases were successfully prosecuted in court. Two of these cases involved chasing the suspects through the woods before they were apprehended. In one of them, after I caught up with the culprit I was threatened with a deadly weapon – but that's another story.

CAR CLOUTING – AN OUTRAGE

You come to the parks to get away from the daily grind, commune with nature, and in general to enjoy yourself, but sometimes that just doesn't work out the way you had hoped. Take for example Pam, a college student at Wake Forest University, who was traveling home from school to Lexington, KY. Since she was about to graduate she took advantage of a long weekend to move some of her belongings from her apartment to her parents home. Her car was crammed full of her clothing and other personal belongings. She had planned to make this a leisurely two day trip so she decided to get off of the interstate and take the scenic route up Rt. 441 through the Great Smoky Mountains National Park. Pam was an avid hiker and had been in the park in the past with her parents, and again on a spring break backpacking trip with some college classmates.

The Smokies was one of her favorite places to be and she had some very fond memories from past hiking trips. Since she had plenty of time, and needed a break from driving, she decided to stop and take a short hike up Alum Cave Trail to the Bluffs, a five mile round trip that takes about two and one half hours. She pulled off into the Alum Cave Bluffs Trailhead at about 1:00 pm. Then she made a classic mistake, she bent down and stuffed her purse, with over $1000 cash in it, under the front passengers' seat.

Pam then grabbed her day pack and a water bottle out of the back and started up the trail. She had a great hike, and had spent some extra time up at Alum Cave area just "kicking back" and enjoying the beautiful day, and returned to the trailhead about three hours later. When she got back to the parking lot she was horrified to find that the passenger side window had been smashed, glass was splattered all over the passenger seat as well as throughout the front compartment of the car and the passenger door was partially ajar. In a panic she checked under the passenger seat and found her **purse gone**. As if this wasn't bad enough she looked in the back seat and found that she had just about been wiped out. All of her clothes were gone, the only clothes she had were on her back. She also found her laptop computer, boom box, and IPod had been stolen.

She tried her cell phone, but there was no coverage in that area, so she drove down the mountain toward Gatlinburg finally getting phone reception just before reaching the Sugarlands Visitor Center (VC). When she finally made contact with 911 they directed the call to the park dispatch center. Dispatch had a ranger meet Pam at the VC. From there they went over the Little River Ranger Station about a mile away to complete a car clout report. The ranger was taking information on the car clout from Pam when I walked into the ranger station. As the District Ranger I had been keeping up with all of the car clouts on the district so I wanted to get the information on this incident first hand. Inside the ranger station I met with Pam, she told me about the break-in and having all of her money, clothing, and other items stolen. She said all she had left were the clothes on her back; she had less than one half tank of gas in her car, had no money, no credit cards, and had over two hundred and fifty miles to go before reaching home. She said that she had planned on getting a motel room in Pigeon Forge, and then really broke down when she realized that she couldn't even change into clean clothes after her hike.

The other ranger was getting the details for the report, and taking care of getting the credit cards cancelled to hopefully prevent the thieves from using them. I guess I was trying to take care of her emotional needs. But I was at a loss on what I could do to help, and then I did the natural thing. I picked up the phone and called Linda, my wife. Pam was about the same size as Linda, and after I explained the situation to her she said she would take care of it. Linda went through her closet and found some things that she thought Pam could use. I left Pam with the ranger to complete the report and said I'd be back in about forty minutes. Sure enough, when I got home Linda had several blouses, skirts, and slacks for me to take back to Pam; another successful team rescue. The clothes may not have been co-ed styles, but when I got back and gave them to Pam I quickly found out that it really didn't matter, she was ecstatic – plus it looked like the clothes would fit. With that taken care of I gave Pam thirty dollars for gas money to get her home. She would send the money back to me, but the clothes were hers' to keep - or pass on to the next needy person.

The term "Car clouting" is used almost exclusively by the National Park Service and other land management agencies to describe the breaking and entering of vehicles, with the intent of stealing items from the inside of the vehicles. The term clout means "to hit", and somewhere over the history of the NPS it became the official term used throughout the Service for incidents involving theft from motor vehicles. Car clouting is one of the crimes that occur in our national parks on all too frequent basis; unfortunately, unwitting park visitors are the victims and because of the lack of knowledge about the potential threat in the parks there are plenty of visitors that have their vacations ruined on their vacations.

The method used by these thieves is normally to set up their operations at park trailheads or parking lots where they know that their unsuspecting victims will be away from their vehicles for a period of time. The thieves range from amateur to professionals and work as individuals and as organized groups working the parks. They often work a circuit of parks within a geographic region, such as, parks in the southeast, east, mid-Atlantic, mid-west, west Coast, etc. The amateurs generally are opportunists looking for a quick way to pick up cash, and the needs for drugs are frequently the reason for the need for cash. Professional car clout groups or gangs are more frequently found working our national parks than is commonly known. These thieves often work in pairs; one person is dropped off and "cases" the vehicles in the parking lot while the other stays with their vehicle. They often use radios to communicate information on the best "targets" and give early warnings if rangers are coming or other visitors are becoming suspicious. The person that is dropped off will often hide in the woods and watch visitors as they leave the vehicle. Another often used method is for the person to walk a dog around the parking lot, looking inconspicuous while watching for potential targets.

Once the clouters have broken into a vehicle or two at a trailhead they almost always leave the area immediately and head toward the park exit. On the way out they will often make a quick stop at another popular trailhead to make a quick hit on other vehicles. If they have gotten credit cards in the stolen items they will almost always head immediately toward major retail stores, such as WalMart, Lowes, or other department stores to use them. If their stolen booty includes a debit card they'll tear the purse or wallets apart looking for a slip of paper with the security pass code on it. In that case, it's straight to the ATM machine to drain the account. NEVER, NEVER keep your security pass code in your purse or wallet with the same credit or debit card.

The vast majority of the car clouts that have occurred in the parks are a result of a purse that has been placed under the car seat when the visitors leave the car. Rangers conduct interviews with car clouters who have been caught breaking into cars in the park. We have learned that in almost every case the clouters are watching for women leaving the vehicle without their purse; often actually seeing them bend down placing the purse under the seat.

So, what do you do to prevent yourself from becoming a car clout victim? First, plan your hike or visit. If you know you are going on a hike prepare for it in advance. If you can, always take your valuables with you on the hike or into the visitor center; if you can't take them with you leave them at home, or some place safe. Never pull up to the trailhead and hide your purse or other valuables in the car; somebody may be watching. A better solution would be to pull off somewhere before getting to the trailhead and place the valuables in the trunk. Women should get in the habit of carrying a small fanny pack or day pack, or make a show of placing valuables in one group pack at the trailhead. If someone is watching this will indicate to them that your valuables are on your person or in the community pack, not in the vehicle.

After a car clouter makes his hit, rangers usually get involved when the visitor arrives at the visitor or the Ranger Station to report the crime. The ranger immediately interviews the victim to get as much information as possible, first to try to get a good description of any suspects, possible vehicles involved, and a direction of travel so the suspects can be stopped before they leave the park. Secondly a report is needed as a way of compiling evidence for future cases as well as for the victim to make an insurance claim. If there is possible suspect and vehicle information the park radio begins to sing, everyone throughout gets into the act to try to identify the suspect vehicle. If credit or debit cards have been stolen the victims are immediately brought to the ranger station where they can make phone calls to have the credit cards cancelled and have a "flag" placed on the cards to see if any new activity occurs on them. Cancelling and having the cards flagged is crucial and must be done immediately, this not only protects the victims from additional charges to their accounts, but it also is a major help in capturing the culprits.

As an example of the magnitude of the car clouting problem, 2003 started off with a bang at Great Smoky Mountains National Park. Before the end of June there were already forty five known car clouts within the park. The modus operandi or "MO" was almost always the same, vehicles at trailheads had their windows smashed out and a purse was stolen from where it had been stashed by the vehicle owners – under the front seat. Most of the clouts occurred at trailheads along Newfound Gap Road (Alum Cave Bluffs Trail, and Chimney Tops

Trail), Little River Road (Laurel Falls Trail), and on Cherokee Orchard Road (Rainbow Falls Trail).

It would seem that after forty five clouting incidents the law enforcement rangers should have been able to stop this illegal activity, or capture the thieves. However, there are at least two major reasons why it is so difficult to get a handle on this activity. 1) LACK OF LAW ENFORCEMENT RANGERS, this is not a whine but a statement of fact. For example, on any given day throughout the year its normal to have only one Law Enforcement Ranger on duty to cover the entire Little River Area. That area includes all of Newfound Gap Road to the NC line, Little River Road to Metcalf Bottoms Picnic Area, Cherokee Orchard Road and Roaring Fork Motor Nature Trail, and the Foothills Parkway Spur between Gatlinburg and Pigeon Forge. That area includes over seventy nine miles of roads, not to mention over two hundred and thirty miles of backcountry trails and one hundred and twenty thousand acres that one ranger (or two if you're lucky) is responsible for during his or her shift. 2) The criminals who do these ill deeds are parasites, but they're smarter than you give them credit for. They do their homework. They spend a lot of time in the park just watching visitor patterns and where law enforcement rangers are positioned, often using a scanner to listen to the police activity in and outside of the park. They are also very smart about not setting a pattern, changing the days of the week and location of the hits, and they often go two weeks or more without making a hit – just to "let it cool down a bit".

If a particular pattern is not apparent it makes it very difficult to determine when and where the clouters are going to hit next. Since Great Smoky Mountains NP is the most visited park in the nation, it also has a high volume of Law Enforcement and other emergency incidents occurring on a daily basis. The protection rangers are often handling multiple calls at one time, so without a particular pattern being determined it makes it almost impossible to pull someone off of patrol to sit on one possible location.

The real answer to this problem is to do the same as what all law enforcement agencies throughout the country do when they have a criminal problem – hire more law enforcement officers to correct the problem. This of course is simpler than it sounds since Congress sets the park budgets. That said, there have been some fantastic criminal cases made over the past ten years in the Great Smoky Mountains NP; for example in 2003 there were two major cases made involving two different car clouting groups. The first actually began with a series of car clouts in late 2002 and continued through the spring of 2003. This case involved a female that was finally linked to thirty five different car clouts in the Great Smoky Mountains NP before she was caught and convicted. The second set of clouters involved three persons, two men and a woman who were finally caught and convicted on ten counts of vehicle larceny that occurred in the park. These three were heavy drug abusers and were hitting vehicles in the park to support their drug habit. The female was a former registered nurse whose drug habit led her on a major crime spree. Don't expect this type of case to develop quickly though, it takes lots of time to piece the physical evidence together, conduct interviews, piece the interviews and physical evidence together from various cases, stakeout potential locations, collect video surveillance from stores where purchases were made, conduct the search and arrest warrants, and prepare for the final indictment and court case.

The bottom line, **BE AWARE** that this problem exists, take precautions and don't become a victim. Unfortunately, there seem to be plenty of these criminals out there. Catch one or a group and it slows it down for a while, but it seems that someone always fills the void after a while. You may do everything right and may still get hit. But, if you do get hit while in the park report it immediately. You may be the link needed to make a significant case and get some of these criminals out of the park. **Help yourself, help your fellow park visitor, and help a Ranger – REPORT CRIMES IMMEDIATELY.**

MANHUNT – THE PURSUIT AND CAPTURE OF ERIC ROBERT RUDOLPH

The public is well aware that Park Rangers are routinely involved in searching for lost persons in our national parks, however, what does not seem to be common knowledge is that there are a relatively large number of "manhunts" for wanted criminals intentionally eluding the law that also occur in the national park areas. Why is this? Well, consider that large national parks, forest, and other federal lands are fairly vast, remote, and typically have a lot less enforcement personnel than city, county, and State law enforcement agencies. If a person wants to "hide out" from the authorities, what better place to go? When you're searching for a lost person they generally want to be found, it makes the job much easier because they are trying to "be found". If they are trying to elude you it makes the job much more difficult, as well as much more dangerous for the "search teams". If a fugitive is the person that is being sought, which naturally adds a real element of danger to the mission, we refer to these teams as "Tactical Tracking Teams".

One of the most famous manhunts that occurred in the Great Smoky Mountains National Park occurred from 1998 to 2003. Eric Robert Rudolph, who was wanted for several murders, led law enforcement agencies on one of the nation's largest manhunts in history. Rudolph was wanted on multiple felony charges stemming from four separate incidents of terrorist bombings from 1996 to 1998. These included the bombing of two abortion clinics, a gay-lesbian bar, and the bombing of Centennial Olympic Park in Atlanta in 1996, which killed two people and injured more than one hundred people.

By the time he was in his thirties, Rudolph was fully immersed in the anti-Semitic and extreme sentiments of the Christian Identity and other extremist groups. Being a loner he followed their rhetoric but never actually joined their ranks, and it is believed he committed all of the attacks on his own without the help of any of the extremist groups. At the age of fifteen he and his mother moved to the Murphy, NC area. He grew up with the mountains of western North Carolina as his playground, and he became friends with a couple of notorious individuals who were survivalist and associated with militia extremist groups. This was a relationship that not only fueled the hatred for anti-Semitic, racial, abortion, and homo-sexuality, but also taught him skills in weapons use and wilderness survival.

In 1998 when authorities identified Rudolph as a prime suspect in these vicious terrorist attacks he fled into the mountains in the western North Carolina area, adjacent to the Great Smoky Mountains National Park. Rudolph was on his old "stomping grounds". He knew the turf so well he spent the next five years in the wilderness near, and perhaps in the park, eluding authorities until May 2003, when he was captured in Murphy, NC. It was later determined that Rudolph had preplanned his "escape" into the mountains so carefully that he had lined up caves, campgrounds and other hideouts in advance, and that he knew the mountains so well he could navigate at night with little problem.

Once authorities realized that Rudolph was probably hiding out in the mountains of Western North Carolina a task force of several Federal, State and local law enforcement agencies was formed solely to locate and capture him. This taskforce was lead by the FBI's Southeast Bomb Taskforce. What is not commonly known is the extent of involvement that the National Park Service, and specifically Law Enforcement Rangers from the Great Smoky Mountains NP (GSMNP), played in the Eric Robert Rudolph case. The fact is, the Rudolph case is the largest manhunt to date on the continent of North America in which National Park Service Law Enforcement Rangers served a major role as tactical man trackers operating in a woodland environment. At the height of the operation in 1998, over one hundred fifty law enforcement officers representing local, state, and federal agencies, conducted daily woodland search and detection patrols, and as many as five law enforcement rangers from the Great Smoky Mountains led the numerous man tracking teams.

In early July of 1998, after Rudolph surfaced in the mountains of western North Carolina, GSMNP Law Enforcement Rangers were assigned as trackers and team leaders for S.W.A.T and ATF teams. Throughout the summer of 1998, five rangers from the North Carolina side of the park cycled through the detail serving as man trackers until the fall of 1998. In addition, from the summer of 1998 through the spring of 1999, one Smokies ranger, who I'll refer to as ranger Pat, was permanently assigned to the Southeast Bomb Taskforce (SEBTF) in Andrews, NC and served as a Tactical Advisor/Lead Tracker/ Liaison. Ranger Pat served as a tracker for the manhunt teams, recording 600+ miles of foot patrols during this phase of the manhunt, and assisted with coordination of the daily ground manhunt operations for Rudolph in the mountains of western North Carolina, including up to ten tactical tracking teams, six FLIR (Forward Looking Infra-red Radar) equipped aircraft, K-9 and bait vehicles. Ranger Pat planned, coordinated and implemented the application of long-term surveillance operations using elite units of the FBI and ATF, and provided weekly operational briefings, focused on the methodology of woodland searching, officer safety, and additional case information, to the search teams that rotated through the manhunt.

After almost a full year of scouring the mountains of western North Carolina for Rudolph from summer 1998 to summer 1999 the teams had failed to capture him. Earlier clues that the teams had developed had gone cold, and it looked as if Rudolph may have escaped, completely leaving the search area. The field searches in the mountains were scaled down and the FBI began to concentrate on other possible locations outside this search area. In order to continue to search the mountains of WNC, the FBI Scout Program was formed. From the fall of 1999 until Rudolph's capture rangers served as consultants and coordinators for the FBI SCOUT Program, responding to and evaluating leads that were developed by the SCOUTS. The SCOUT program was a group of off-duty law enforcement officers who camped in areas that Rudolph was known to have frequented. The SCOUT teams continued to develop evidence that he was probably still in the area, kept pressure on Rudolph, and kept him on the move. Then suddenly, on May 31, 2003 police officer J.S. Postell, a 21-year-old rookie in the Murphy Police Department, NC found Rudolph rummaging through a trash dumpster behind Save-A-Lot supermarket. Postell arrested him on the spot sparking a long chain of legal events and interviews.

While it is true that these teams did not capture Rudolph during these manhunt operations, they were instrumental in locating evidence of his activity in the area, several of his campsites, and in the end some of the four explosive caches he had in the area. It was later determined by the FBI that they were very close on several occasions, and the pressure that they put on him by the Ranger led SCOUT Teams kept him on the move and unable to carry out further attacks. One of these caches found later contained two hundred fifty pounds of nitro glycerin based dynamite. According to FBI Executive Assistant Director Chris Swecker, who headed the Charlotte office when the arrest was made, "Rudolph admitted that he'd toyed with going after the agents who were pursuing him. We know he buried at least four caches of explosives in the area. One was right above the National Guard armory where our command post was located. He claimed he made the decision not to booby-trap our post. But I think he didn't because we kept the pressure on him, kept patrols going, kept a visible presence. He just couldn't get to his explosives and do what he would have liked to have done. That was the primary reason we were there. We wanted to catch him, but we also wanted to make sure he didn't strike again. I'm convinced that the investment of manpower we had during that time period saved lives."

In 2003, after Rudolph's capture, ranger Pat and another ranger were reassigned full-time for the purpose of locating Rudolph's camps, caches, and searching for additional evidence for prosecution. This post capture searching would help in several ways. To collect evidence for the upcoming trials, to show the effectiveness of the search teams during the heart of the fugitive search operations, to better understand the mind of a fugitive being sought by the authorities, and to help in answering questions for an after action review. A review of the operations would enable law enforcement officials to learn from their mistakes as well as their successes.

Rudolph wasn't doing a lot of talking, but after a plea agreement was reached in April 2005 he did tell authorities of the location of two camps and caches that he had in the area. Armed with this information, three rangers worked as scouts on missions that recovered over two hundred fifty pounds of dynamite and other bomb making equipment buried at multiple locations throughout western North Carolina. At one location, which Rudolph called his "winter camp", a little-used section of the Nantahala National Forest in the Fire's Creek recreation area a large food cache of grain and a Belgian made .223 FN/FAL assault rifle was recovered.

The degree of danger to all who worked the manhunt, along with the physical and psychological demands of hunting for someone who has already taken human life, and is likely ready to take yours, was unbelievably stressful work. The amount of respect that our rangers received from the other agencies involved was tremendous. As Ranger Pat commented, "Prior to this time I had pretty much taken our skills for granted... It was through watching my constituents apply their craft in contrast to the other agencies that made me realize the uniqueness of being a ranger and the value of our skills. This is not in any way meant to diminish the skill of any other agencies because most of them were working outside of their normal environment. Our contribution to this case set a precedent for the utilization of land management agencies that will have far reaching affect on enforcement efforts in our country in the future."

The events came to a conclusion on April 12, 2005 with the trials in Birmingham and Atlanta; the involved rangers were to see Rudolph sentenced to serve four life sentences. Because Rudolph is no longer talking about his escape into the mountains, many questions remain on how he did it. Other question also still remain, such as, are there anymore weapons and explosive caches still out there, and was Rudolph ever actually in the Great Smoky Mountains National Park? On the latter, and according to ranger Pat, "maybe", there was never any positive proof uncovered that he was in the park, but there is at least a strong possibility.

THIEVERY - AN ELECTRIFYING EXPERIENCE

So what is it with some people? Ever notice how some people work so hard to get out of work? Most people find work rewarding, you get a distinct sense of satisfaction knowing that you have completed a task. Unfortunately not everyone subscribes to this same work ethic. Most of the thieves I have ever dealt with are like that, they seem to work a lot harder to get out of work than if they were to get a real job and make an honest living.

Then you have those folks that may actually hold an honest job, but are always looking for some easy money, even if it means breaking the law. Sometimes the route to that easy money can be a lot more costly than it would have ever been if they had just run a straight course. During my time at New River Gorge National River I met many local people that were always looking for an easy way to make a buck, mostly through illegal activities. Some of these folks would steal anything that wasn't nailed down. It didn't matter what it was, as long as it was "free" for the taking. I've worked cases of stolen rocks, stolen junk, stolen timber, stolen signs, stolen fence post, items stolen off of buildings, you name it and I've probably seen it stolen.

Take for instance a man from Mount Hope, WV, we'll call him Greg. It was late November 1998 during deer season and Greg decided that he would take his six year old son with him while he went deer hunting. Since hunting in the park is authorized this was an appropriate activity, but taking his six year old son with him during deer season, without taking proper safety precautions, may require some debate as to his judgment on the matter. Anyway, he and his son left their home and walked into the Garden Ground area adjacent to the park. Greg and his son were walking along an old electrical power line about one mile from his home when he decided that instead of deer hunting he would turn this outing into a cash making experience, that "easy money" thing.

Well, what do you think Greg could have found worth stealing out here in the woods? Remember when I said he was walking along an electrical power line? Yep, you guessed it, there's copper up on those electrical lines. Seeing an opportunity, Greg took up his high powered rifle and began shooting at the high tension power lines, which unfortunately was the main line servicing the Mount Hope area. After several tries at shooting the base of the line at the insulator junction he hit it, the line came down and Greg was electrocuted.

According to his six year old son his daddy told him to go up the hill and stay out of the way. Greg then started to shoot at the power lines and insulators with the rifle. The live power line came down and either hit the ground near Greg or landed directly on him. Greg was wearing steel toed boots, which aided the electrical conduction, because he had an entry wound on the foot and an exit wound on his head. The 6 year old boy said that he heard his daddy scream, and told investigators that the "wire bit him". The boy went over to his father, found him unresponsive and wandered around the wooded area for about one hour, until a hunter found him and reported the incident to 911.

The investigation showed that this wasn't a "one shot deal"; perhaps greed for a bigger fortune got in the way, because we found another location along the power line about two hundred yards from where Greg's body was found where one hundred feet of high tension copper wire had been recently removed. Beside where we found Greg's body we also found a roll of copper wire about one hundred feet long that matched the wire missing from the location two hundred yards away.

The theft of copper wire is a common target for thieves in that area; they often go to great lengths to steal it and then sell it to local scrap dealers. Of course receiving stolen property is illegal, even in West Virginia! And it makes sense to me that even a scrap dealer might find electrical copper wire, the type from a main high tension power line, highly suspect as being stolen property. The State Police and local authorities do team up to run "sting" operations on this type of illegal activity, the main reason is to protect the property of others, but as you see it could also help to protect the thieves themselves. It's just too bad that Greg didn't get a chance to learn this lesson by an encounter with law enforcement authorities; instead he paid with his life.

I guess the saving grace in this particular instance is that Greg had enough sense to have his six year old son stand back out of the way while he shot the power lines down. Greg died because of his greed and his mistakes, but his son could have died just as well – remember he ran to his fathers side after he was electrocuted. You have to wonder, was it luck or a miracle, or was it maybe divine intervention that saved the child?

INCIDENT MANAGEMENT

"What can Brown do for you?"

"The primary goals of the NPS are to safeguard human life, safeguard the resources from permanent or lasting damage and to safeguard public and personal property. As the primary law enforcement and emergency operations entity in national parks, park rangers are regularly involved in all aspects of emergency operations including law enforcement, search & rescue, emergency medical services, wildland & structural fire, and responding to natural disasters."
-- NPS Emergency Management Capabilities And National Response Plan Responsibilities,

FIRE AND INCIDENT
MANAGEMENT OPERATIONS

The concept of managing emergencies using the Incident Command System can trace its roots from the United States Military. During World War II our military used a form of the command system that allowed it to coordinate and manage the immense war machine that spanned the globe. After World War II the nations wildland firefighting agencies developed a national fire management system using the model based on the successes shown by the military during the war. In the 1970's a series of large wildfires occurred in southern California which resulted in numerous problems. These problems were mostly a result of poor communications and lack of a common system of management by the several State, Local, and Federal agencies that were involved in the management of the incident. This sparked an interagency task force called FIRESCOPE that looked into the issues. As a result of this review the Incident Command System (ICS) was put into effect on all wildland firefighting operations national wide. Since the 1980's the ICS has been used almost exclusively in wildland firefighting as the method of managing large complex fires.

Following the 9/11 attack on the World Trade Center the Federal Emergency Management Agency (FEMA) was put in charge of developing and managing the ICS to include all emergencies. This is now referred to as "All-Hazard" incident management. But All Hazard incident management did not start with FEMA, many federal and state organizations were using the Incident Command System to manage all emergency incidents since it was introduced in the early 1980's. In the late1980's the National Park Service coined the name of "All – Risk" incident management and has used it religiously since then. It was, and still is, used for every type of emergency incident large and small and includes incidents in law enforcement, fire, EMS, search and rescue, traffic accidents, hurricanes, floods, tornados, demonstrations, planned special events, and even large and complex planning operations.

Firefighting is a part of every Protection Rangers duties, it can involve wildland, structural, or vehicle fire depending on the park they are assigned to and may involve detail assignments to parks, forest and other federal and state lands.

The National Park Service protection ranger wears many hats, with the core responsibility being LE, SAR, EMS, and Fire. But what is not common knowledge is the extent that the rangers have been involved in the ICS from the beginning of the management system. I got my start in incident management even before I began my career with the NPS, as a seasonal firefighter with the U.S. Forest Service. I continued to be deeply involved in wildland firefighting after moving over to the NPS in 1979, initially working fires in the park and on special fire assignment throughout the U.S.

Over the course of over thirty five years as a wildland firefighter I have worked on fires in nineteen states ranging from the east coast of South Carolina to the west coast in California. Every fire I have been on has been notable in one way or another, but the most memorial for me was the Yellowstone NP fires of 1988. The Yellowstone fires are considered a milestone in the national wildland firefighting arena for several reasons. From June 14th through September 11th this complex of fifty one fires burned a total of 793,880 acres inside the park and over 500,000 acres outside the park. This was one of the largest firefighting efforts in the history of the United States. It involved over 25,000 people and over $120 million was spent in the firefighting efforts. The operational lessons learned, both positive and negative, were considerable and had a dramatic affect on the future of national fire management. In addition to the operational lessons, fires in the 1988 Yellowstone Complex virtually rewrote the book on using fire as a tool for managing the forest ecology. This fire assignment also had a dramatic affect on me personally and on my professional growth as a wildland firefighter. This was a very complex and challenging thirty day assignment and was conducted at an exhausting pace. As a young crew boss assigned to the Mammoth and North Fork Fires I was in charge of a twenty person fire crew. This assignment involved working both inside of Yellowstone NP and the Targhee National Forest, most of the time in true wilderness situations. There were numerous obstacles to overcome during this assignment including lack of equipment, lack of personnel, encounters with wildlife, environmental factors, safety issues, communications issues, shear exhaustion, and of course too much fire. But the experiences and lessons learned were invaluable and have paid off in dividends over the course of my career.

Rangers are expected to be involved in wildland firefighting at their home park, but it is usually optional for them to take an assignment to fires and other incidents outside of their home unit. For me personally, firefighting, and emergency management activities as a whole, are activities I enjoy. Therefore throughout my career I have actively pursued being involved in all emergency management incidents.

In the 1980's the National Park Service developed Special Event and Tactical Teams (SETT), primarily to manage the law enforcement component of incidents on large operations like special events, demonstrations, fugitive incidents, hostage incidents, and other law enforcement emergencies that occur throughout the U.S. Most of the eight regions in the NPS have a SETT team, and in 1987 I was selected as the SETT leader for the Mid-Atlantic Region (MAR) of the NPS. As the SETT leader for MAR I was responsible for a group of eight rangers, and from 1987 until 1992 we worked several incidents including special events at Yorktown NHP and several events at Independence NHP, a marijuana cultivation surveillance operate at Delaware Water Gap NRA, a poaching operation at Shenandoah NP, and a sting operation at Petersburg NHP to correct a problem with homosexual solicitation in some of the outlying areas of the park.

HURRICANE ANDREW: In 1992 my SETT team was detailed to Everglades NP in response to Hurricane Andrew as one of several SETT teams that would manage security throughout the park. After our arrival it was determined that there were already more than enough security personnel on the incident. Andrew was a huge incident and in addition to the Everglades NP the incident management team was also responsible for the management of all recovery efforts in Big Cypress Preserve and Biscayne National Park. The three parks had not only lost a number of building, utilities, and other infrastructure, but they had also lost hundreds of navigational aids, such as buoys and channel markers on the inland and coastal waterways. Since several rangers on my team were certified boat operators and scuba divers it was only natural that we would be assigned to Biscayne NP to help manage the coastal rehabilitation operations.

Rick Brown as the "Harbor Master" in his outdoor office at Biscayne NP during recovery operations for Hurricane Andrew in 1992.

We spent three weeks at Biscayne and Everglades managing the parks boat flotilla to deliver work crews, researchers, and supplies to barrier islands for cleanup, and in the stabilization, reconstruction projects, performing cleanup, reconstruction on various structures on the mainland and the islands, and since the park land and waters were closed – performing law enforcement duties. The teams' scuba divers worked with crews replacing navigational aids and with researchers to document resource damage and resource impacts.

There were hundreds of persons assigned to the incident and as the group supervisor I was responsible for between 15 to 30 persons, depending on the number of crews assigned on a given day. The work was demanding, especially because of the variety of tasks involved. The days were long, stressful and strenuous, and the demands placed on the group with limited resources were steep.

Even with the demands and high expectations placed on us it didn't take long for us to realize how lucky were to get this assignment instead of the security detail. The rangers assigned to the security detail were mainly assigned to stand long hours at gates or other stationary positions, or running patrols in parks that were closed to the public. Our team was intimately involved in the operation and we were doing a large part in putting these parks back in order – it was a great feeling.

After the three week detail I returned home to my normal position at New River Gorge National River. Two weeks later I was asked to return to Everglades NP to serve on the Incident Management Team as the Operations Section Chief. On this assignment I was responsible for all of the Hurricane Andrew operations for all three parks. I had been involved in incident management teams on wildland fires, and numerous other smaller incidents for several years, but this was my introduction to major incident management from an "All Risk" standpoint. I truly enjoyed solving the problems and in being a part of putting things back in order after a major incident. This was the beginning of a change in direction in my professional development. From this point on I would be a part of incident management for the NPS on a national scale.

After the Hurricane Andrew detail I decided it was time to leave the SETT detail and pursue a position on the NPS All Risk Incident Management Teams. The National Park Service Northeast, Southeast, and National Capital Regions combined together to form one All-Risk Incident Management Team (ARM). I applied for and was selected as the Operations Section Chief for the team.

I served as the Operation Section Chief on the NPS Eastern "ARM" Team for several years. As the Operations Section Chief I served several assignments, including **OPERATION BRIDLE TRAIL**, a double homicide that occurred in Shenandoah National Park in 1996. This incident involved two women who were murdered in their tent while camping on the Appalachian Trail. The NPS worked the incident jointly with the FBI. In 1997 the Eastern IMT was assigned to **HIGHWATER 97A**, which involved a major flood in the Yosemite Valley of Yosemite National Park. This flood resulted in major destruction that cost over $300 million to repair. In 2001 I served as the Deputy Incident Commander on the **NEW RIVER FLOOD**, a major flooding incident involving the New River and several surrounding towns.

In the spring of 2001 I was selected as the Incident Commander (IC) for the NPS Eastern Incident Management Team. The Eastern Incident Management Team actually consisted of two separate teams at the time. They rotated on assignments but still found that they were too busy with out of park assignments. These out of park details took them away from their primary jobs and their families so it was decided to add a third team to help distribute the workload. I was one of three IC's on the Eastern Team and my first responsibility was to put together another full team from other qualified personnel in the three regions. It took several months to fill out the team with qualified personnel, but by later summer of 2001 we had a team together and were ready for assignments. Each team was named after the IC, so we would be known as the "Brown Team".

9/11 TERRORIST RESPONSE

After fleshing out the team roster it didn't take us too long to get our first assignment. On the morning of September 11, 2001 I was at Fayette Station below the New River Gorge Bridge with the Teams Planning section Chief. We were beginning the process of putting together an Incident Action Plan for the upcoming "Bridge Day Event" when I received a radio call to get to a telephone immediately. I went to my office on the gorge rim where I called park headquarters and found out that the World Trade Center had been bombed by terrorists. Like everyone else we found a television and were glued to it all morning to get details on the incident. Within three hours I received a telephone call from the Northeast Regional Office in Philadelphia; the "Brown Team" had been activated and was to report to the Northeast Regional Office in Philly, immediately. Planes throughout the country were grounded for fear of additional terrorist attacks so there was no possibility of flying to Philly. After quickly packing my bags I was on the road that afternoon driving to Philly. The following morning the Brown Team mustered in the NE Regional Office Philadelphia to begin our first team assignment.

Our mission was to develop and implement a plan to identify how the NPS would respond to terrorist threats in our Icon Parks in the Northeast Region. The parks we were responsible for included, the Statue of Liberty, Ellis Island, Gateway NRA, The Manhattan

Sites which included Federal Hall NM, Castle Clinton NM, Theodore Roosevelt Birthplace NHS, General Grant NM, St. Paul's Church, Independence NP (with the Liberty Bell and numerous other icons), Boston NHP (with the USS Constitution and numerous other historic sites). We had to identify what the potential threats were and how we would secure them. We would have to set priorities between the sites and notify and activate SETT teams and additional Protection Rangers to secure the sites. In addition, there was an immediate operational component to the incident, to assist the parks and park personnel in New York near "ground zero". These sites included The Statue of Liberty NM, Ellis Island NM, Gateway NRA, and the Manhattan Sites. The park personnel at these sites had been involved in the initial response to the attack or were traumatized by the attack in a number of ways; they needed outside help. We put together and implemented the plan to address the security issues for the entire Northeast Region, conducted on-site visits to the Statue of Liberty, Ellis Island, and some of the Manhattan Sites, and worked with the Regional Director to arrange meetings with the staffs of the parks near "ground zero" to address their immediate issues.

T-5 TORNADO

On April 29, 2002 a category 5 tornado hit the Charles County area of eastern Maryland. Six people were killed in the tornado and damage was estimated in the millions in and around La Plata, Md. Thomas Stone National Historic Site is located just a few miles from LaPlata, Maryland and the tornado had passed through the park causing extensive damage to the small historic park. The destruction to the park included major tree damage, damage to the historic Thomas Stone residence, and the total destruction of all of the buildings in the park maintenance facility.

On April 30 the Brown Team was activated to respond to the hurricane. We arrived on May 1 and began work on the damage assessment and a recovery plan. There was major damage to the park facilities but luckily, because this was a small park, most of the damage was confined to a relatively small area. We ordered tree working crews with bucket trucks from other parks to clear trees from the roadways and trim out hazardous limbs. We also brought in additional skilled maintenance workers from other parks to help with carpentry, electrical, and plumbing repairs. In addition to the skilled workers we also able to get a thirty person AmeriCorps Crew out of Washington, D.C. to work on debris cleanup and the removal of destroyed buildings. With these emergency workers it took only five days before we had the park back to relatively good shape. On May 6th the Incident Management Team was able to hand the remaining repairs back over the park to continue the rehabilitation.

The aftermath of the T-5 Tornado on the park maintenance area at Thomas Stone National Historic Site.

JULY 4TH EVENT and the GRAND OPENING of the NATIONAL CONSTITUTION CENTER AT INDEPENDENCE NATIONAL PARK

In July 2003 the Brown Team was detailed to manage the July 4th celebration at Independence NP (INDE) in Philadelphia, PA, which would culminate with the opening of a new facility managed by a NPS/ Park Partner, The National Constitution Center (NCC). Prior to this event I had worked several assignments at Independence. There were always a bunch of really 'interesting twists' to an event at "INDE", especially the demonstrations that happened even during normal times. But this was July 4th after 9/11 so it was anyone's guess what we might face. Our mission was to develop a plan and manage all of the incidents involving the July 4th celebration. We were also tasked to work with the NCC staff to assure the NCC was ready for the event (the huge building was still under construction right up to the last minute), and to manage the grand opening ceremony. In addition, we knew that there would be demonstrations, especially on July 4th. that would impact and change our plan, therefore contingencies had to be built into the planning.

During the week leading up to July 4th we managed several smaller events without a hitch. The day of July 4th was a bit more interesting with several major demonstrations through the streets around the NCC. During one of the marches the parade route was altered by the demonstrators and they entered a closed street in front of the podium area and tried to overrun the ceremony site and the entrance to the NCC. The aggressive demonstration group was pushed back by the rangers and Philadelphia police officers that were manning the site and two demonstrators were arrested.

There were several important dignitaries attending the ceremony, including three U.S. Supreme Court Justices, the Governor of PA, Mayor of Philadelphia, and Director of the NPS. During the NCC dedication ceremony a large arch that the NCC staff erected as a prop at the last minute tore loose from its guy-wires and fell on several of the dignitaries. Seven VIP's were injured, and Justice Sandra Day O'Connor narrowly escaped injury. Except for the threat from the demonstrators and the arch falling on the VIP's the event went very well. There were several really scary possibilities that could have happened, including terrorist incidents, that didn't happen. We had contingency plans in place for all number of possible twists that could occur, luckily none of those plans were necessary.

HURRICANE RESPONSE

There are several National Park areas on the east coast, gulf coast, and of course Florida. Because of the major hurricane threat along these coasts it stands to reason that the Eastern Incident Management Team would get the majority of hurricane assignments. The years between 2003 and 2005 were bad hurricane years for the entire area and the Brown Team was assigned to manage four different hurricane assignments during this three year period.

HURRICANE ISABEL Sept 18 – Oct 5, 2003

Hurricane Isabel began as a tropical wave off the coast of Africa on September 1st. It strengthened to a Category 5 hurricane on September 11th with maximum sustained winds estimated at 145 knots. Luckily as it turned away from Bermuda it began to weaken and on September 18th it made landfall near Drum Inlet, NC as a Category 2 hurricane. The entire Outer Banks region of North Carolina took a hard hit. The hurricane then moved inland and weakened to a tropical storm. It moved into southern Virginia taking down trees, powerlines and creating all sorts of havoc.

The NPS activated three incident management teams to handle the problems. One team to Colonial National Historical Park in VA, one team to manage the destruction at Richmond NBP, Petersburg NB, and Fredericksburg NMP in Virginia and the Brown Team was directed to

manage the destruction on the Outer Banks parks, this included both Cape
Hatteras National Seashore and Cape Lookout National Seashore.

These two parks on the North Carolina coast comprise virtually
all of the Outer Banks, and from north to south the area spans
a distance of about one hundred miles. It would be the teams'
responsibility to manage all of the hurricane related issues on all of
the National Park lands within that one hundred forty mile stretch.
Just about every park area saw significant damage, including the
Wright Brothers NM in Kitty Hawk, NC, Fort Raleigh NHS and
Park Headquarters in Manteo, NC, Bodie Island Light House, Bodie
Island Maintenance buildings and Ranger Station, Oregon Inlet
Campground, Cape Point Campground, Ocracoke Campground,
Frisco Campground, Cape Hatteras Lighthouse, Cape Hatteras Coast
Guard Office/Ranger Station, Buxton Ranger Station/Maintenance
Area, Ocracoke Island Ranger Station, Ocracoke Light House. We
would also be responsible for rebuilding the Ocracoke Pony Pens,
cleanup of Ocracoke Campground, stabilization and rebuilding of
beach access ramps throughout the park, sand management, repair of
the Ferry Landings at Hatteras and Ocracoke Islands.

In addition to the huge amount of work we faced we also had several
major challenges to overcome, like the fact that the bridge to Hatteras
Island and all of the ferry landings had been knocked out by the hurricane.
Not only was it a challenge getting emergency personnel to the islands of
Hatteras, Ocracoke, and Cape Lookout, but getting supplies and materials
there was almost insurmountable. We also faced a very political problem
of sand management with the local communities. The controversial issue
of whether or not the dunes would be rebuilt on NPS owned beachfront
to protect private development had to be sorted out and managed.

Hurricane related issues we faced at Cape Lookout NS included
significant damage to the Historic Portsmouth Village (Life Saving
Service Station, School, and Historic Cemetery), ferry landings at
Shackleford Banks, Great Island, Long Point, and Portsmouth Village,
and Cape Lookout Lighthouse. All of these areas required cleanup and
stabilization. We also had recreational vehicles that had been destroyed

or stranded at the camper village at North Core Banks. All of these vehicles had to be removed from the island before they caused addition damage to the resource. While dealing with the rehab operations we were also called on to assist NC State in rounding up the wild ponies on the islands for testing and vaccinating for equine encephalitis, and had to deal with a plane that crashed within the national seashore.

To say that we had our hands full would be a bit of an understatement. We were overwhelmed with the amount of destruction and the task to put it in order. Transportation from one end of the incident to the next was a major hurdle. Luckily the park had a park pilot with a small plane and helicopter that could be used to move the key incident staff around. The aircraft and pilot were also a major help in assessing damage on the incident and setting priorities for work projects. After a three week assignment the Brown Team rotated out and transitioned the incident to another NPS Incident Management Team. That team worked on the incident for three more weeks before turning it back over to the park to continue the recovery efforts.

HURRICANE IVAN Sept 18 – Oct 2, 2004

Ivan was a classical, long-lived Cape Verde hurricane that developed from a large tropical wave that moved off the west coast of Africa on August 31, 2004. It reached Category 5 strength three times before it finally made landfall as a 105 knot Category 3 hurricane on September 16, just west of Gulf Shores, Alabama. By this time, the eye diameter had increased to forty to fifty nautical miles, which resulted in some of the strongest winds occurring over a narrow area near the southern Alabama and western Florida panhandle border. This was just a few miles west of the headquarters of Gulf Islands National Seashore in Gulf Breeze, FL. A storm surge of ten to fifteen feet occurred along the coasts from Destin in the Florida panhandle westward to Mobile Bay/Baldwin County, Alabama. A possible record wave height observation of fifty two and a half feet was reported by the NOAA Buoy in the north central Gulf of Mexico south of Alabama. Extreme rainfall totals exceeded fifteen inches along the coastal Florida panhandle near Pensacola and the Alabama border.

After making landfall the storm continued inland and caused flooding, tornados and other destruction as far north as Pennsylvania. The forces of Ivan were directly responsible for ninety two deaths, twenty five in the United States. Ivan caused extensive damage to coastal and inland areas of the United States. Portions of the Interstate 10 bridge system across Pensacola Bay, Florida were severely damaged in several locations as a result of severe wave action on top of the ten to fifteen feet storm surge. As much as a quarter-mile of the bridge collapsed into the bay. The U.S Highway 90 Causeway across the northern part of the bay was also heavily damaged. To the south of Pensacola, Florida, Perdido Key bore the brunt of Ivan's fury and was essentially leveled. In short, Ivan was the most destructive hurricane to affect this area in more than one hundred years. At one point, more than 1.8 million people were without power in nine southern states.

On September 18th the Brown Team was activated to respond to Gulf Islands National Seashore in Gulf Breeze, FL to deal with the aftermath of the hurricane. The team arrived on September 18th and found the area completely without electricity, telephone service, and the park radio repeaters. The only area within the park left standing was the park maintenance area. We set to work getting generators, cellular phones for our immediate office equipment needs, and for communications within the team. The only housing available for the team was in Destin. The hurricane had knocked the bridge out between Destin and Gulf Breeze making it an hour and a half hour drive to get to park headquarters each day.

After taking care of our immediate needs for office space the team began damage assessments and putting together an Incident Action Plan (IAP). The plan would address a wide variety of projects that would be taken on by the team. These included the removal of hundreds of trees that had been blown down and uprooted, mounds of trash deposited on shoreline and into shoreline vegetation near park headquarters, the stabilization and reconstruction of the Park Headquarters building (it had suffered major water and structural damage), and the stabilization and reconstruction to the Fort Pickens buildings. Fort Pickens also had major damage to curatorial exhibits and storage facilities, park offices, maintenance facilities, a curatorial storage facility that had been destroyed, and several historic buildings that had been damaged by the high surf and winds. There was also park vehicles and law enforcement equipment damaged or destroyed in salt water surge. To complicate things the road to Ft. Pickens was destroyed. We would have to move all personnel and supplies and equipment to Fort Pickens either by boat or by helicopter. In all, the hurricane recovery estimate reached sixty-five million dollars.

Fire crews were brought in to clear trees and manage the debris removal. Heavy equipment was brought in from other parks and contractors were utilized for the heavy removal. Maintenance crews were brought in to repair damaged buildings, specialized hazmat contracts were arranged to take care of specific problems with mold from flooding. Boom trucks and chippers were brought in with crews from other parks to clear trees off building and trim hazards. Specialized teams of cultural and natural resource specialists were also brought in to manage sensitive resource issues and to preserve the damaged artifacts and collections. The Brown Team managed the incident for two weeks, and on October 2nd we were relieved by another NPS Incident Management team. The second team continued the recovery efforts for two additional weeks before transitioning the incident back to the park to manage.

HURRICANE KATRINA Sept 1 – 21 and Sept 29 – Oct 15, 2005

Hurricane Katrina was one of the strongest hurricanes to impact the coast of the United States during the last one hundred years. When Katrina entered the warm waters of the Gulf of Mexico, it quickly began to strengthen and became a Category 5 hurricane with winds over one hundred fifty five mph and eventually reached a peak intensity of one hundred seventy five mph. It made landfall in Plaquemines Parish in Louisiana at 6 a.m. on August 29th with winds of one hundred forty mph. As the storm continued north it made a second landfall near the Louisiana/Mississippi border at 10 a.m. with winds of nearly one hundred twenty five mph. The storm weakened as it moved inland, but it was still a hurricane one hundred miles from the coast.

Katrina caused widespread devastation along the central Gulf Coast states, with cities like New Orleans, La., Mobile, Ala., and Gulfport, MS being particularly hard hit by Katrina's force. Katrina struck the coastal areas of Louisiana, Mississippi, Alabama and Florida on August 29, 2005 causing an incredible amount of damage to the Mississippi District of Gulf Islands National Seashore. Hurricane Katrina was the fifth in a series of storms to ravage Gulf Islands NS in the past twelve months. Katrina served another damaging blow just as Gulf Islands NS struggled to rebuild after being hit hard by Hurricane Ivan just under a year ago, followed by Tropical Storms Arlene and Cindy, plus the impacts of Hurricane Dennis as recently as July.

On September 1, 2005 Team Brown of the Eastern Incident Management Team was assigned to manage the hurricane aftermath at Gulf Islands National Seashore. It was almost impossible to get airline flights into the Pensacola area, so most of the team members drove down from various parks from throughout the Northeast and Southeast Regions. As we drove down we started seeing hurricane damage as far north as Mobile, AL. It got progressively worse the further south we went but nothing prepared us for the destruction we found when we drove into Ocean Springs, Mississippi, the home of the Mississippi District of Gulf Islands NS. The damage was incredible, each of us had our own thoughts on what we would find facing us in the park. It didn't take long to find out, as we started down the entrance road to the park we found it completely choked with trees across the road. Luckily, there had been some local residents who lived on roads off of the entrance road who had cut a narrow path into the road. We were finally able to weave our way through the road to the park maintenance area/ranger station. When we finally got to the maintenance area we were pleasantly surprised to find that even though there was some building damage, most of it was intact. However, there was no electricity, water, sewage, or telephone service to the area. Because of the massive damage and the lack of electricity in Ocean Springs and the surrounding area, there was no available lodging or restaurants in the area for the teams' use. Therefore, we made camp at the maintenance area using the buildings for shelter. Luckily we came prepared with food and camping equipment for a week. We also set up our Incident Command Post (ICP) at the maintenance area. We brought in generators, a satellite cellular telephone trailer, portable toilets, charcoal grills and had a decent camp set up for the incoming crew personnel.

We started assessing the damage to the park, and found that all of the buildings on the Davis Bayou mainland area, with the exception of the maintenance area, had been either destroyed or severely damaged. This included the Visitor Center, five park residences, the government boat dock and the public boat dock, and the campground. We found that the ranger station, ranger residence, and maintenance area on Horn Island were completely destroyed. The ranger residence and all public use facilities on Ship Island were destroyed, and Ft. Massachusetts had been over washed by the storm surge and sustained damage and needed extensive cleanup and stabilization. We also found that the park employees on the Mississippi District had sustained considerable damage to their homes; they needed physical as well as emotional support to get them back on their feet and back to work. Our plan addressed employee assistance and assistance to park neighbors as priority areas.

Entrance road to the Davis Bayou Unit of the Gulf Islands National Seashore as it looked when the team first arrived on the Katrina Recovery.

Entrance road to the Davis Bayou Unit of Gulf Islands NS after a week of cleanup efforts by the team. Most of the facilities in the area, including park employee residences, park visitor center, and the campground were completely destroyed or suffered heavy damage. The road clearing was only one of several rehabilitation jobs that were occurring at the time the photo was taken.

After a three week assignment the Brown Team was relieved by another NPS Incident Management Team from the Western Region, who continued with hurricane rehab projects that we had started. We went back to our normal jobs and lives for two weeks, and on September 29, the Brown Team returned to re-assume management of the incident. After the second rotation we transitioned the incident to a smaller incident management team that was left in place to finish up loose ends. In the thirty four days we served on the Katrina detail we completed the following projects:

- Conducted two hundred sixty NPS Employees Assistance projects, which included help to twenty six employees, seventy two volunteers, and over two hundred park neighbors over the period of the incident.

- Debris cleanup in the Davis Bayou area. Set up temporary office trailers for park employees, including installing electricity, phone and computer connectivity.
- Demolition of the Visitor Center Skiff Dock/Boardwalk.
- Repairs to the Campground Boardwalk (using salvaged materials).
- Construction of two temporary storage/shop buildings at the Government Dock.
- Stabilization of the Government Boat Dock.
- Cleanup and debris and tree removal from the Davis Bayou Campground, with hundreds of trees removed, chipped and hauled away.
- Worked with FEMA to move forty seven residential trailers for displaced families into the Park Campground. The campground was used as a long term housing area for displaced families.
- Completed repairs and established electricity, water, and sewage to all fifty two campsites in the Campground.
- Completed repairs to the Campground Office.
- Installed two washer and dryers for employee use in the Campground.
- Stabilized and repaired the severely damaged public restroom at the Public Boat Dock.
- Assisted the park IT Specialist in re-establishing park phone system and computer connectivity.
- Cleaned up debris in Ft. Massachusetts.
- Rebuilt doors and windows in Ft. Massachusetts.
- Cleaned up shoreline debris from East and West Ship Islands.
- Cleaned up two miles of debris near boat dock on Horn Island.
- Gutted and rebuilt interiors of three NPS residences in Davis Bayou area.

- Wrote contract specifications for several contracts including the rebuilding of the Government Boat Dock, Ship and Horn Island Piers, destruction and removal of building debris from Horn Island, shoreline debris removal, and asbestos removal from two houses.
- Ordered and set up trailers and constructed a wooden ramp on the trailers to be used as a temporary Visitor Center.
- Created six new full hookup trailer sites (sewage, electricity, water) on Boat Launch Road for NPS employee use.
- Repaired the foot bridge near the campground *(a safety hazard for the residents of the FEMA housing area in the campground; it was cheaper to repair than remove).*

The National Park Service has used the Incident Command System to manage just about every form of emergency and non-emergency incident imaginable. On a regional and national level the NPS has used the ICS with specially trained incident management teams to manage numerous major incidents including:

- Hurricanes
- Floods
- Wildland fires
- Search and Rescue Operations
- Presidential visits and vacations
- Special events
- Two Olympic events (Atlanta Summer Olympics and Salt Lake City Winter Olympics)
- Administrative incidents such as, (Operation Opportunity – the downsizing of the NPS, fugitive searches, Transition of the Presidio of San Francisco from the U. S. Army to the National Park Service, Y2K – to coordinate responses to problems potentially generated by the change of the century)
- Barricaded subjects and hostage incidents

- Hazardous Materials and Oil spills (Exxon Valdez oil spill and numerous others)
- Terrorist Events (such as, Security response to 9/11 attack on WTC, Operation Liberty Shield, security activities at icon parks related to the beginning of the war in Iraq, July 4th events involving security at icon parks)
- Large Gatherings (such as, World Unity Fest - a Rainbow Family event, Sturgis Motorcycle Rally)
- Dedication of newly authorized NPS sites
- Cruise Ship Grounding at Glacier Bay National Park.
- Tower Demolition - the demolition of the National
- Tower at Gettysburg National Military Park.
- Centennial of Flight - event at Dayton Aviation Heritage National Historical Park and at Wright Brothers National Memorial
- Funerals for NPS Line of Duty Deaths

At the park level the Incident Command System is used almost exclusively to manage everything from a motor vehicle accident to the dedication of a new visitor facility. In short the NPS has just about made an art form out of using the ICS. The projects completed on the incidents described above represent an incredible amount of work accomplished in a short time period. This is possible when working with a highly motivated and skilled team, when provided the funding, and when given the trust and support of upper management to help cut through the red tape and bureaucracy. Another key is that when a team is assigned to an incident they can concentrate only on the task in front of them. Their normal jobs back in the park are left for others to take care, they come to an incident with a clean slate prepared to work hard and get the job done.

The Eastern NPS Incident Team AKA "the Brown Team" taken at Gulf Islands National Seashore during the 2005 Katrina Recovery incident. This was a milestone in the recovery process, after two weeks of cleanup and rehab work the UPS made its first delivery; hence it was a lighter moment for the team. After the team photo in front of the UPS truck the team motto of "What can Brown do for you" was born.

BRIDGE DAY AT NEW RIVER GORGE

Some may ask "what in the world is a Bridge Day"?. But by now most folks have seen or heard of it in some form or another. Over the past thirty years Bridge Day has been on National news on several occasions. Numerous newspaper and magazine articles have been written and several magazine and television documentaries have been produced about the event. Bridge Day is the one day out of the year, usually the third Saturday of October that the bridge is open to pedestrian traffic, parachutists can legally jump from the New River Gorge Bridge, and other unusual high adventure activities are permitted to happen. Over the past thirty years Bridge Day has become a major celebration, a State holiday, and a huge boost to the local and State economy.

The bridge has two lanes going north and two going south with a concrete barrier dividing the north-south lanes. There is not a pedestrian walkway on the bridge so it is normally closed to pedestrian traffic. When the construction of the Bridge was completed on the October 22, 1977 the governor held a dedication ceremony in which he invited the public to walk across the bridge. Opening the bridge to pedestrians would mean closing at least one side of the bridge, a major disruption to the normal traffic flow. Therefore it was not intended at the time for this "bridge walk" to be an annual event, but it has somehow worked out that way. There has been a Bridge Day event on the bridge every year since 1977, with the exception of 2001. That year, after the terrorist bombing of the World Trade Center the Bridge Day Commission decided to cancel the event because of possible terrorist threats.

The New River Gorge Bridge on the annual Bridge Day event, crowds of over 200,000 people are common to watch the BASE Jumping and partake in the other events.

The bridge is State property, but it adjoins to National Park Service property, the New River Gorge National River, on both sides of the river. The bridge foundation on either side of the river and the land directly under the bridge is the only part of the land that is owned by the State of WV, everything else below and to the sides of the bridge is NPS property. Any activity that occurs on the bridge is not the concern of the NPS, but if the activity occurs in any way on NPS property it is the concern and responsibility of the NPS. And just about every major activity that occurs on Bridge Day ends up on NPS property.

At a distance of three thousand thirty feet from rim to rim the New River Gorge Bridge is the second longest single arch bridge in the world. It is probably most famous for the parachuting, or B.A.S.E. Jumping, that occurs annually from the bridge on Bridge Day. B.A.S.E stands for Building-Antenna-Span-Earth. Parachutists jump from these structures normally using a "ram air" self inflating style of parachute to arrest their fall. Obviously it takes a high structure as a launch site to parachute from and the New River Gorge Bridge qualifies at eight hundred seventy six feet from the deck of the bridge to the river below.

The first recorded B.A.S.E. jump occurred in 1912 when Frederick Law parachuted from the Statue of Liberty. There were several other famous "platforms" used as launch sites through the years. Most of these jumps were made illegally, like the first B.A.S.E. jump from El Capitan in Yosemite National Park in 1966. Modern B.A.S.E. jumping goes back to 1978 when a documentary was made using the new ram air parachute to jump from El Capitan in Yosemite NP. BASE jumping continued in popularity over the years, and today it is a well known extreme sport.

The popularity of Bridge Day also has increased, from the first walk across the bridge on opening day in 1977 when several hundred attended the opening ceremony, to today where Bridge Day draws an estimated crowd of about 200,000 people. The New River Gorge National River was established as a unit of the National Park Service in 1978. It took a few years for the park to put together a management staff and become operational in the area. By the time the park was somewhat operational Bridge Day had already become established as a local event, and was beginning to get national attention. In 1979 the first BASE jump was made from the bridge, that "outrageous" act generated so much attention that in 1980 officials from the local Fayette County Chamber of Commerce came up with the idea of establishing the annual Bridge Day.

Bridge Day was off and running now and nothing could hold it back. In 1981 rappelling from the bridge was added to the agenda with several ropes set up from the catwalk under the bridge. The rappelling groups set the ropes up at intervals across the bridge, with the ropes increasing in length as they reached the middle of the bridge. The longest rappel was over five hundred feet; the rappellers would descend the rope then climb back up to the catwalk on mechanical ascenders. This of course took time, and it was soon realized that the ropes interfered with and caused grave safety issues from the parachutists. By 1981 commercial river outfitters got into the act and established "mini" rafting traps that they launched just upstream from the parachute landing area. They ran a couple of rapids in the rafts and then would just hang out in the rafts watching the Bridge Day activities. In addition, entertainment, food sales, and commercial booths on the bridge were added to the agenda. It was quickly turning into a real "circus".

In 1983, after seeing the change in the event and with concern for the future impacts, the National Park Service became involved in working with the Chamber of Commerce to manage the event. This would hopefully help to correct the increase in illegal BASE jumping and guide the event in a positive direction. That year spectators coming to the event increased dramatically and there was also major friction that occurred between the BASE jumpers, bungee jumpers, and rappellers. Bridge Day 1983 also saw numerous injuries to BASE jumpers and the first BASE jumping fatality occurred during the Bridge Day event. The death was a result of drowning because there was no river rescue available for the event. With the increase in popularity, the conflicts between the user groups, the injuries, and a death that occurred on National Park Service property the park had to get more involved, even if they didn't have an operational staff on site at the time.

I transferred to New River Gorge in the spring of1985, I only had a few months to get ready for and experience my first Bridge Day. As the first, and only, field Protection Ranger in the park I was little more than an observer that year. This year brought increased crowds that were estimated at over 100,000, traffic problems, over-taxed local law enforcement, and an increase in BASE jumping with two hundred fifty registered BASE jumpers who made six hundred fifty jumps. High winds also hampered the jumpers this year causing several injuries. Luckily most were broken or sprained ankles. Another issue also became apparent; the rappel ropes out in the middle of the bridge were causing a huge safety problem for both parachutist and rappellers. When the jumpers exited the bridge and deployed their parachutes the high winds would blow them back into the rappel lines. There were several near miss incidents when a parachutist was blown into the ropes, risking parachute entanglement in the ropes, and on one occasion the parachutist actually hitting the rappeller, almost knocking him off the rope. I learned a lot from the experience that I would use over the next fifteen Bridge Day events. My main contributions that year were working with the BASE Association to help get a river rescue operation established (a very capable local whitewater outfitter in motorized boats was contracted to pluck jumpers out of the river), and working with local law enforcement to help manage the crowds.

BASE jumper makes a water landing after a jump from the New River Gorge Bridge.

In 1986, in an effort to improve the overall safety and efficiency of the event the park began a planning effort several months before Bridge Day. BASE jumpers had already had a tragic accident this year. In August five Canadians staged an illegal jump one evening from the bridge and one of them landed in the river and drowned. I learned a pretty valuable lesson from this incident, that this group could be really cut throat. When the one jumper landed in the river, went under and didn't come up, the rest of the group realized he was probably dead so they just fled the scene. One member of the group did call in to the local Sheriff Office a couple hours later and report the drowning, so at least we had some information to go on. I was able to get re-contact information on the reporting party and did finally get more information so we could launch an effective search of the river. But since the jumper was sucked down by the swift river current we weren't going to find him until the gasses in the body floated it, as it normally turns out that was three days later. The other three jumpers in the party simply left the area that night and went back to Canada. We never did have contact with them, only the one person that was good enough to report the incident. Of course the reporting party denied that he had jumped, saying that he was just along to watch, but we later found out that he was one of the jumpers.

This incident underscored our conviction that we needed to work with the BASE Association and the local community to have one legal day for BASE jumpers to jump off of the bridge. The bridge was already a huge draw for BASE jumpers and we were beginning to get illegal jumps on several occasions throughout the year. By having one day that we could hold a legal jump, we could plan the event, put in safety measures for river and land based rescue, and EMS to make jumping from the bridge as safe as possible. We also knew that the vast majority of BASE jumpers were respectable and morally correct people who did not want to break the law. We hoped that they would encourage the few "bandit" jumpers to save their jumps for Bridge Day each year for the overall benefit of the sport.

Since "Aerial Delivery", basically landing an aircraft or parachute on park property is illegal unless permitted by the Park Superintendent the park agreed to issue a permit to the BASE Association. They could jump from the bridge without NPS approval, but there was not any place except for NPS jurisdiction to land, so to do this legally we needed to issue a permit. We began planning for the event several months ahead and involved the Chamber of Commerce, local law enforcement, the BASE Association, the leaders from the rappelling group, the river outfitter that served as river rescue the previous year, and the other twenty two commercial river outfitters that used the area. We also established an Incident Command System for the event, and I served as the Incident Commander for the activities that occurred on NPS property.

The park had hired a few extra seasonal river patrol positions for the 1986 season, so during Bridge Day we were able to put an NPS boat on the river to help with picking up parachutists that landed in the river. With the high winds the previous year there were several times when parachutists were blown downriver near the head of the "Fleaflicker Rapid". The outfitter boat had a hard time getting to those jumpers before they were pulled downriver by the current of the rapid, so we positioned our boat and crew just below the rapid. This way we could run upstream into the rapid or downstream as needed. It would free up the primary rescue boat to concentrate on the more frequent rescues upstream in the main pool, and give us an extra margin of safety downriver.

Our operational plan for the landing area included EMS, River Rescue, Land Rescue, Crowd Control, Safety of Spectators, and Monitoring the Permit to assure jumpers were adhering to the safety guidelines that were established. That year the park certainly didn't have enough rangers to work every angle of the event so we incorporated local law enforcement, and volunteer groups. A local commercial ambulance company volunteered to station two ambulances with paramedics at the Parachute Landing Area at Fayette Station. For river rescue we had the commercial outfitter as the primary pickoff boat with the NPS boat downstream. We also used several volunteer fireman stationed on both sides of the river with throw ropes that could be thrown to jumpers who landed near shore and to serve as first responders to spectator injuries. Our primary rescue group consisted on only four rangers and our problems included water rescue, tree rescue, cliff rescue, and rescue from powerlines. Not much for the potential number of incidents, but it was a beginning.

Bridge Day was also another one of our "family affairs". My wife Linda was a Surgery Nurse at the local hospital, so on Bridge Day she was always on call. Almost every patient we treated at the parachute landing zone, and on the bridge would go to the local hospital. Most of those were orthopedic cases and she was involved in their surgery. That was the way it was for the remainder of our seventeen year stay at New River, and that went not only for Bridge Day but for any incident throughout the year.

Rangers and medics transport an injured BASE Jumper to the medical staging area after landing on the rocky shoreline on opposite side of the river

As Bridge Day got underway that year we had plenty of business for the surgery staff. The day was really windy and was playing havoc on the jumpers landing on the ground at Fayette Station. Most of the experienced jumpers tried to stay out of the river so they could keep their parachute dry; that way they could make a quick trip back to the top and jump again. The erratic winds were causing hard landings and we had several broken and sprained ankles, and broken arms that occurred throughout the day. And then at about 1:45pm the real injuries began to happen. One of the most experienced jumpers at the event, who was also on the safety committee from the BASE Association, jumped later in the afternoon after working hard all day to make the event as safe as possible. Unfortunately, when he jumped his parachute went into a spiral, the wind caught him and blew him off course and he came down hard right onto a huge rock on the shoreline, narrowly missing a group of spectators on the rock. He hit the rock with his legs first causing a major femur fracture and numerous other injuries. He then bounced off the rock and fell into the river. I was standing at the landing zone about forty yards away when he hit the rock and I heard the loud crack from his leg fracturing. It was a sickening sound. Even though he was close to shore he was in water about ten feet deep and the current was swift. Drowning was a real concern, but we were able to reach him by the motorboat as well as from shore before he went under or was pulled downstream by the current. He was placed on a backboard, stabilized and transported by ambulance to a medical helicopter waiting at the top of the gorge, and then on to the hospital. The jumping was stopped while we took care of this critical patient and after about thirty minutes it resumed.

And then at 2:38pm a 27 year old man, who had made numerous jumps from the bridge that day, jumped his final time. He held his pilot chute longer than normal and when he finally made his release it deployed from the pack but did not open. The chute simply streamed behind him unopened. He pulled his reserve chute when he was about one hundred fifty feet above the water. It also deployed but did not have time to open before he splashed into the river below. He had gone straight down from the bridge without gliding at all and landed under the bridge at the upper end of Fleaficker Rapid. When he impacted the river immediately the water turned completely red where he went in, and then the current from the rapid caught him and he was swept downriver through the rapid. I was between the launch area and the rapid when he landed, about fifty yards from his landing point. The noise from the impact was like a gunshot going off. The rangers in the NPS boat were in the right place to grab him as he was swept downriver. They pulled him into their boat within a minute of his impact, but when they pulled him into the boat they knew that he was already dead. His back had split open on impact with the river, draining his entire body of blood. In the follow up investigation we learned that this jumper was apparently on a mission to make as many jumps as possible that day, maybe to set some kind of record. On his next to the last jump he apparently had landed in the river, got his parachute wet, but did not allow it to dry out before repacking it. He then jumped with a wet parachute, not a good idea. This was a safety issue that had been addressed and was covered by BASE and the NPS in the safety briefing and literature that was distributed to the jumpers and it was being driven home to the jumpers throughout the day. But we also knew that it was the responsibility of the individual jumpers to pack their own parachute. If someone was determined to pack a wet chute there was really no way to police it.

This was just one of many valuable lessons we learned during this year's event. In future events we would recommend having a more secure parachute packing area where safety riggers could be on hand to assist and give closer guidance. Another major safety issue that was identified was several jumpers had launched on their own from locations other than the designated launch zone, sometimes multiple jumpers at a time. This was extremely dangerous because they could collide, or otherwise interfere with the person jumping from the designated zone, potentially causing injury or death to both parties. It also made rescue at the bottom very difficult. The rescuers at the bottom were in communication with the launch zone at the top, coordinating so the rescuers were ready for the jumper; when the bandits went off there was no way of knowing it on the bottom before they jumped. Several of these bandit jumpers did get in trouble on their landing because of their misdeed. We would incorporate tighter controls in future events.

The 1988 Bridge Day was one of the safest in the history of the event, apparently the lessons learned and applied paid off. As the annual Bridge Day continued over years we continued to learn and improve the safety for the event. The safety issues were monumental, and it seemed that each year we learned of other issues we needed to address. Take for example the main line CSX Railroad tracks that run on both sides of the river in the bridge area. Trains run on schedule, and they don't stop because of an event like Bridge Day. It would be tragic if a parachutist jumped from the bridge just as a train was coming down the tracks and landed on or in front of the train. Our early measures were to put out spotters to give us an early warning of an approaching train, then we would stop all jumping until the train cleared the area. Over the next couple of years we were finally able to convince CSX to station railroad officials at Bridge Day along the tracks near the landing zone to coordinate with us. This worked out great because they had the train schedules and also had direct radio communications with the trains. They were also law enforcement agents and could help to enforce the closures along the train tracks to keep spectators clear.

Another issue we dealt with on the train tracks was entanglement in the power lines and the potential for electrocution. The power lines run continuously along the tracks to supply the lights and switches, and they are charged with 440 volts of electricity; enough to fry a person wrapped up in them in a parachute. A parachutist could potentially hang in the lines and not get shocked as long as they weren't touching the ground and the lines at the same time. If an unknowing rescuer touched a jumper entangled in the powerlines it grounded him and they could both get fried. So this became an issue of educating the rescuers, the jumpers, and coordinating with CSX to cut the power if necessary.

One of the goriest accidents that I observed, and was a first responder on, was a result of a landing on the railroad tracks in 1999. Bridge Day 1999 turned out to be a windy day, jumpers were having trouble landing at the designated LZ near the river takeout, and were getting blown off course and landing near the railroad tracks throughout the day. Near the end of the day one jumper was blown toward the railroad tracks. His only landing options were to land on the railroad tracks, in the trees, or into the rock embankment uphill of the tracks. He chose the tracks and lined up to land in line with the tracks, but he was coming in hard and out of control. When he came in for his landing he clipped the power lines. The parachute hitting the power lines spun him perpendicular to the tracks and when his feet touched down they both slipped under the railroad tracks. As I mentioned, he was coming in hard, so when his feet got trapped under the tracks his feet stopped immediately, but because of his forward momentum his body didn't. Both legs from the knees down were almost literally ripped off of his body; the only thing holding them on was badly damaged muscle and other soft tissue.

Its unfortunate, but Injuries were just part of the Bridge Day event. The jumpers were aware of the risk, and the rescuers knew what they were facing each year. Some years went very smoothly with only minor injuries, but some were absolute mayhem; we never knew what we would get, we just prepared for the worse case scenario. The weather and elements had a lot to do with how safe the event was each year; wind, rain and high water played havoc on jumper safety, sunny and calm days were generally fairly safe for jumping. There have been several deaths as a result of BASE jumping from the bridge, but so far only three deaths have occurred on Bridge Day itself. Those were the 1983 drowning when river rescue wasn't available, the 1986 incident, and most recently one that that occurred in 2006. The death in 2006 happened to a very experienced BASE jumper who had trouble deploying his pilot chute; this of course prevented his main parachute from opening before he hit the river.

BASE jumping has always been the main attraction on Bridge Day, and the area where the NPS rangers and other rescuers concentrated on for obvious reasons, but it wasn't the only concerns we had to deal with. With 200,000 people at an event we also had crowd control issues, traffic issues, law enforcement issues and rescue of the general public to contend with. Most of the spectators were on the bridge itself, but many were at the landing area and crawling all over rock cliffs to get a good view of the BASE jumping activities. This of course meant that we would potentially have spectators falling off of cliffs and other high places, and we did have falling accidents on several occasions during my sixteen Bridge Day events.

Because of the crowds and traffic problems, there was no way that a team from the bottom could respond to an accident on top of the gorge in a timely manner, so we had to develop an additional rescue team for incidents that occurred in the rim area. That of course meant spreading our scarce resources over a very wide area. It was a lot of responsibility and took a lot of planning and coordination. For an emergency service provider Bridge Day is an event that has about anything one could ask for. On this one day out of the year there is probably no other event in the world that surpasses the technical expertise that is needed to address the ever changing situations. You can go from an incident involving law enforcement, to rescue, to emergency medical, to interpreter in an instance. It involved a lot of skill and practice.

In the early days of the event, because of scarce resources, we could only provide a very limited EMS service at the bottom. By 1994 we had a full blown MASH unit station at the parachute landing area at Fayette Station. This unit included an orthopedic surgeon, several nurses, and several paramedics. Today that unit has expanded even further and several lives have been saved because of the caliber of medical service provided on site.

It doesn't just stop with Bridge Day though; the bridge itself seems to have a life of its own. There were several other spectacular events that occurred on the New River Gorge Bridge during my time there, including:

KAT MANDU: Bridge Day 1985 was one of distinction not only for the normal crazy Bridge Day activities but for the fact that Astronaut Jon McBride was a special guest to the annual event. In addition to Jon McBride, Kat Mandu, a well known stunt performer was geared up to perform a death defying escape from a locked wooden box that was to be set on fire while it was dangled over the bridge by a crane. The stunt turned out to be a no-go; it was cancelled because of communication problems, but only after causing huge problems resulting in delays and coordination problems with the BASE jumpers and rappelling groups.

TRUCK BUNGEE: On July 24th 1992 a Los Angeles based film company filmed a bungee "jump" of a GMC Jimmy truck from the New River Gorge Bridge. A ramp was set up that hung over the edge of the bridge railing and would tip the truck off of the bridge. A huge bungee cord that was about 12 inches in diameter was attached to the rear of the truck, and the truck was released to take its plunge over the bridge. After the truck was dropped a worker was lowered over the side on a crane, a cable was attached and the crane hauled the truck back to the top of the bridge.

This stunt was performed for a thirty second commercial that would show the toughness of the GMC truck. The stunt worked like a charm and it was definitely spectacular. Describing makes it seem simple, but the behind the scenes dynamics were complex and involved. It took weeks for the film company to convince the Dept. of Highways that the stunt wouldn't damage the bridge. Once convinced they had to overcome the issues of stopping traffic and traffic control before they obtained the permit from the State. Then they had to work with the National Park Service for the filming permit since the stunt would actually be filmed from NPS property. Then visitor safety had to be taken into consideration. Besides the large film crew, State engineers, local law enforcement for traffic control and security, the National Park Service had 10 employees involved in the filming to monitor the film permit and address safety. I served as the Incident Commander for the NPS portion of the event, which meant working with the filming crew and multiple other agencies to take care of visitor safety. We set up boat safeties below the bridge, stopped river rafting traffic, and kept the general public out of the area when the stunt was taking place.

World Rafting Championships were held on the New and Gauley Rivers on September 22nd through 25th 2001. There were sixteen men's and women's teams participating in the competition, these competitors represented 12 countries from around the world. This was the first international sporting event held in the U.S. since the September 11th terrorist attacks. Because of the concern for terrorism at the time there were several agencies involved in making this a safe and secure event, and since the event was held on NPS jurisdiction the National Park Service served as the lead agency for all security on both the New and Gauley Rivers. The competition involved three days of raft racing on the New and Gauley rivers. The first day involved time trials and a head to head sprint through Fayette Station Rapid on the New River. The second day was a slalom course requiring competitors to negotiate gates hung over the river at several locations on the Fayette Station Rapid. The third and last day culminated in a downriver race on the Gauley River. The Gauley River is one of the most technical challenging and demanding rivers in the U.S. It is rated as a Class V+ whitewater river. During September each year the U.S. Army Corps of Engineers normally releases 2,800 cubic feet per second (CFS) from the dam for whitewater boating. For this event they released 4,000 CFS making this event challenging even for world class rafters. Most of the teams flipped their rafts at least once in the rapids over the course. Four National Park Service rangers paddled a raft as sweep/safety, as well as one ranger who paddled a safety kayak and made numerous rescues over the course. The German men's team and Czech Republic women's team won the world championships. The park's Incident Management Team and the Special Event Team were invited to the final awards ceremony where West Virginia Governor Bob Wise publicly thanked the National Park Service employees for making it a safe and outstanding event.

AFTERWORD:

As you can see, a ranger has to wear a lot of hats over the course of his or her career. Of course the different types of jobs a certain ranger may have to be proficient in will vary depending on the park they are assigned to and the position he is in within that park. A ranger may start out with no experience in technical rope rescue. But if he transfers to a park with high cliffs, caves, rugged terrain, or steep mountain roads where accidents occur frequently then that ranger will have to become proficient in technical rescue. Same goes for a ranger who may be working in a park where his skills are mainly concentrated on rescue or emergency medical work. If he transfers to a park where the main emphasis is on traffic control he will have to quickly become as skilled in traffic enforcement and investigations as any State Trooper.

Over the course of my career I have had to be very proficient in just about every skill known to the ranger profession and to other emergency response and public service professions. These skills include front country law enforcement, backcountry law enforcement, drug enforcement, wildlife enforcement, wildlife manager, cultural resource enforcement, cultural resource manager, rope rescue technician, search technician, cave rescue technician, whitewater technician, whitewater boater, motorboat operator, tactical tracker, emergency medical technician, incident management, disaster recovery, equestrian, hazardous material technician, wildland firefighter/manager, structural firefighter, backcountry management, campground management, educator, public speaker, counselor, fee collection manager, auditor, technical writer, researcher, supervisor, and manager. The list is long, but the rewards are many.

Some rangers excel by being multi-talented; some excel by concentrating their efforts on one or two specialties. Regardless, almost all rangers excel and are extremely talented professionals. No other law enforcement or emergency service agency that I am aware of requires their personnel to wear as many hats and to be proficient in them. However, because of the diversity found within the National Park Service from one park to another having a deep well of skills to pull from is extremely important. A ranger with designs on moving around the nation from park to park, and up the chain of command to supervisor or manager, is almost always much more capable of understanding and managing the wide array of issues that tend to crop up in our National Parks.

As a ranger one of the most frequent questions I have been asked is "how do you become a National Park Ranger"? The most important thing to remember is to get an education, it's almost impossible to get hired initially without a college degree. Once you get your first position you still have to apply and compete for transfers if you want to move on to other parks and up in position. I have applied for a number of jobs over my career only to be beat out by another applicant with a higher degree. It's not uncommon to be competing for entry level jobs or transfers with other applicants who have a master's degree or higher. The bottom line is to stay in school and complete your bachelors' degree at a minimum. For more detailed information on how to become a National Park Ranger check out the website at http://www.nps.gov/personnel/rangers.htm.

You can get additional information on jobs and other aspects of the National Park Service at the following websites:

- Association of National Park Rangers at http://www.anpr.org/

- International Ranger Federation at http://www.int-ranger. net/
- National Parks and Conservation Association at http://www. npca.org/

Also remember, other Federal agencies also have park ranger or similar positions you may want to check out. These include the U.S. Forest Service, Bureau of Land Management, Fish and Wildlife Service, U.S. Army Corps of Engineers, and Bureau of Indian Affairs. And don't forget that State Parks are another source for park ranger positions. Every State has a State Park System so start by checking websites or other sources for these positions.

I truly hope you enjoyed this book and I would like to hear from you with any comments you may have. If you have questions or I can be of help in any way please feel free to contact me at greatsmoky@charter. net. All comments on the book or questions are appreciated.

Finally if you find yourself feeling blue, having a difficult time with something, wanting to quit, or just whining about life in general, just say 'RANGER UP!' If nothing else it may make you laugh; laughter helps almost any situation.

Rick Brown served for 30 years in the National Park Service as a Protection Ranger, retiring in 2007. During his career he worked in four different National Park areas in permanent assignments, and in numerous other National Parks, and National Forest on temporary emergency details. Over the course of his career he served as a field ranger, supervisory park ranger, served as the Assistant Chief Ranger at New River Gorge National River, served in several acting assignments at New River Gorge NR and Great Smoky Mountains NP as Chief Park Ranger, and ended his career as the Assistant Chief Ranger at Great Smoky Mountains National Park. He received numerous awards during his career for exceptional performance, Special Achievement Awards, Exemplary Act Awards for Search and Rescue and Law Enforcement missions. He also received the U.S Dept. of Interior Valor Award (the highest award for valor in the DOI), and was selected as the recipient of the National Harry Yount - Ranger of the Year Award for 2004 (the highest award for National Park Protection Rangers in the National Park Service).

He currently is a part time instructor in the National Park Service approved Seasonal Law Enforcement Training Academy at Southwestern Community College in Franklin, NC, a Swiftwater and Technical Rope Rescue Instructor, and is working for the U.S. Army Corps of Engineers Disaster Response Team as an emergency response specialist.

OTHER RECOMMENDED READING:

Burnett, Jim. Hey Ranger!: Taylor Trade, 2005.

Burnett, Jim. Hey Ranger 2: Taylor Trade, 2007.

Bytnar, Bruce W. A Park Ranger's Life: Thirty-two Years Protecting Our National Parks: Wheatmark, 2009

Farabee, Charles R. Death, Daring, and Disaster: Search and Rescue in the National Parks: Roberts Rinehart, 1998.

Farabee, Charles R. National Park Ranger: An American Icon: Roberts Rinehart, 2003.

McCarter, Dwight and Ronald G. Schmidt. Lost! A Ranger's Journal of Search and Rescue: Graphicom Press, 1998.

Muleady-Mecham, Nancy Eileen. Park Ranger, True Stories From A Ranger's Career in America's National Parks: Vishnu Temple, 2004.

Made in the USA
Lexington, KY
29 March 2014